PRIVILEGED INFORMATION

Contents

Personal Finance

10 WAYS TO BEAT THE BANKS BEFORE THEY BEAT YOU

People are intimidated by banks. They treat bankers as clergymen and banks as an extension of the federal government. Before deregulation, this attitude didn't matter much, because costs to the customer were pretty much the same from bank to bank. After deregulation, however, banks quickly began to vary widely in their services and in the costs of those services.

In order to turn the best profit, banks depend on the fact that customers don't know what to ask for.

Deal with the smallest bank you can find. After deregulation most large banks decided to get rid of smaller depositors. Although this is a blatant violation of a bank's charter—which is granted on condition that the bank serve the whole community— large banks systematically ignored their public responsibility by tacking on higher charges for smaller accounts. They found it cheaper to service one corporate account than 10 individual accounts. The smaller bank, on the other hand, is more responsive to the individual depositor because it needs his business.

Ask about checking accounts:
• What is the minimum-balance requirement? How does the bank calculate it? Watch out for a minimum-balance calculation that uses the lowest balance for the month. Best: A figure based on the average daily balance.
• Does the balance on other accounts count toward the checking-account minimum balance?
• What is the clearing policy for deposits? This is especially important if you have a NOW account. Most banks hold checks 10–14 days, which means you lose interest and may be stuck with overdrafts.
• What is the overdraft charge? Often it is outrageous. In my area of the Midwest, most banks charge $20.

Don't buy loan insurance from the bank. Credit life or disability insurance is often routinely included on loan forms and added to the cost of your loan. Read carefully, and make sure you don't sign any such policy when you take out a loan. This insurance benefits the bank—not you. It covers the bank for the balance of your loan should you die or become disabled. You can get more coverage from an insurance agent for half (or even less) of what the bank charges.

Avoid installment loans. These loans are front-end loaded: Even though your balance is declining, you're still paying interest on the original balance throughout the term of the loan. Ask for a single-payment note with simple interest and monthly payments. If you do have an installment loan, don't pay it off early—this actually adds to its real cost.

Pay attention to interest computation. Most people compare rates and assume higher is better. But it's conceivable that with certain methods 9.75% will actually earn more interest than 10%. What to look for: Interest figured on a day-of-deposit-to-day-of-withdrawal basis, compounded daily.

Avoid cash machines. The farther bankers can keep you from their tellers and loan officers, the more money they'll make and the less responsive they'll be to your needs. Bankers like machines because people can't argue with them.

Negotiate interest rates. This sounds simple, but it means combating banks' tendencies to lump loans in categories—commercial mortgage, retail, etc. For example, banks offer a long-time depositor the same interest rate on a car loan as they do a complete new-comer. But all it takes to get a better rate is is to say, "I think my car loan should be 2% lower. I've been banking here for 15 years, and I have $10,000 in my savings account."

Forget FDIC security. Elderly people are often concerned with FDIC security. Given the option of higher interest rate investment with an equally secure major corporation that probably has more reserves than FDIC, they'll opt for the bank investment because of FDIC insurance. But the FDIC has only $16 billion in reserves. That's a minuscule portion of the money it's insuring. Now that more and more banks are closing every year, the FDIC may soon find itself in big trouble.

Ignore the bank's amortization schedule for mortgages. When you make your monthly payment, especially in the early part of your mortgage, very little goes toward the principal. However, if you choose to pay a small amount extra every month, this will go toward the principal and save you an enormous amount of money.

Example: Let's say you have a $100,000 mortgage at 15% for 29 years. If you make an additional $50 payment per month for 20 years, your 29-year mortgage will be paid off in full at the end of those 20 years. You will have invested $12,000 to save $122,000, and you won't have to make payments over the last nine years.

Don't put all your money in one certificate of deposit. Now that you can deposit as little as $1,000 for the money-market rate, split your deposits. Elderly people, especially, tend to put their money into a $10,000 or $20,000 CD. Then they find they need to take out $1,000 or $2,000. But when they cash large CD, they pay a horrendous penalty. Solution: Instead of buying one $10,000 CD, have the bank write out 10 $1,000 CDs. This way you'll get the same interest and more liquidity.

Source: Edward F. Mrkvicka Jr., a former banker president and author of *Battle Your Bank and Win,* William Morrow & Co., 105 Madison Ave., New York 10016. He now runs Reliance Enterprises, Inc., a consumer advocacy organization that helps individuals recover what banks owe them, Box 413, Marengo, IL 60152.

HIDDEN BANK FEES

• Hidden bank fees vary widely from bank to bank. Examples: A recent survey found that penalties for bounced checks range from $7 to $20. Some banks place service charges on savings accounts that drop below $200, while others set no minimum balance requirements. Bottom line: When shopping around for a bank, take into consideration fees as well as interest rates.

Source: Survey by Consumer Federation of America in *Physician's Management.*

OVERCOMING A BAD CREDIT RATING

A bad credit rating may not ruin your chances for a loan. Be honest about it. Volunteer information about past problems to your loan officer. Then demonstrate how you've changed (with copies of your latest credit-card bills and canceled checks). Any omission will make you appear deceitful when the bank finds out, as it inevitably will. Also: Seek out a senior loan officer (vice president or higher). Reason: Junior officers have less latitude in making questionable loans.

Source: *Sylvia Porter's Personal Finance,* 380 Lexington Ave., New York 10017.

BORROWING ON YOUR HOME

• A home equity credit line is available from most banks and stockbrokers. This arrangement is more flexible than the traditonal second mortgage. Advantage: You draw funds only when you need them and don't pay interest until then.

• Real estate is more liquid than most people think. Although you can't withdraw your investment on a day's notice, you can easily borrow on your equity. And any holding is saleable at the right price. Best bet: A condominium or apartment building in a neighborhood that's appreciating. Then you can afford to sell below market value and still make a profit.

• Refinanced mortgages can make sense for homeowners who borrowed at higher rates than prevail today. General rule: The new interest charge should be at least two points below the rate of the existing loan (to cover the cost of new closing fees and title search). Drawback: Banks often refinance only at variable rates, rather than at fixed rates.

Source: Barry Clements, vice president of Citibank and chairman of the residential mortgage committee of the New York State Bankers Association.

• Repay most loans as quickly as you can. But don't rush with low-interest (student) loans or mixed-rate mortgage, even one as high as 13%. That mortgage is an asset because it's so one-sided. If interest rates drop, you can refinance, but if rates soar, the bank is stricter with you.

Source: Andrew Tobias, author of *The Invisible Bankers* writing in *Parade.*

DANGERS OF CO-SIGNING A LOAN

Three out of four co-signers have to pay in the end. If you decide to co-sign, establish a limit to the amount you'd have to pay in case of default (just the principal balance, for example). And make sure you'll be notified immediately if the borrower misses payment. Best: Resist pressures to sign quickly.

WHAT BANKS DON'T TELL YOU ABOUT CREDIT CARDS

• A department store customer tried to use his VISA card from a local bank. The store called the bank to verify the charge. It was told not to extend credit but to pick up the card instead. The customer sued the bank, claiming the bank's records of his account were in error. The court dismissed the case, saying it made no difference whether the bank's records were right or wrong, as the bank was under no duty whatsoever to extend credit. A credit card is simply an open offer to extend credit. It can be revoked at any time and for any reason—or for no reason.

Source: *Smith v. Federated Department Stores and First National Bank,* 301 S.E. 2d 652.

• Credit-card issuers such as banks, often retain the right to a "security interest" in any purchase. This means they can repossess the goods if payments aren't made as required. The store where the item was purchased will not seek payment, since the credit-card company has already paid them.

• Credit cards do not add all that much onto the average price tab—actually less than 1%, if a 103-page government report is correct. The surprisingly small impact weakens arguments for a dual pricing system designed to protect cash users from shouldering the extra cost of credit-card transactions.

Source: Federal Reserve Board.

HOW TO GET THE MOST FROM YOUR CREDIT CARD

Credit cards have become a way of life for most Americans. However, very few people realize the unnecessary costs they incur by not utilizing their cards to their advantage or by not choosing the least expensive card.

Determine which card is best for you. Banks offering VISA or MasterCard services have a wide variety of fees and interest charges. Some levy a $35 charge while others will nick you for only $5 or $10. Moreover, interest charges for goods purchased range from 14% to 22%. Some banks charge interest from the date of purchase; others charge no interest if you pay your monthly bill on time.

Watch out, too, for bank cards that bill on a 24-day cycle, which means 14 bills per year. If you pay all your bills once a month, one of those 14 could easily get delayed in the shuffle. Then you will be charged interest on the missed bill and earn an undeserved reputation as a slow payer.

Even if you like the credit terms and service charges, find out if there is any time limit on them. Some banks offer attractive deals as part of a special promotion. Take advantage of such offers—but be ready to switch over to another bank card if it is less expensive once the promotion expires.

Credit cards also can be used as a bargaining chip to receive a discount from a merchant. Merchants typically pay a fee of 2%–7% of your charge when you use your credit card. With an American Express of Diners Club card, they may have to wait a while to get paid. It may be to the advantage of the merchant to go along with your suggestion of a 5% discount if you pay cash.

Another idea: Take a cash advance on your credit card, and pay directly for goods and services, rather than charging them. Most bank-interest charges are less (up to 6% less) for cash advances. If you already are being charged interest for purchases, take a cash advance and switch the balance due to the lower rate.

If no interest charge has yet been levied, then time the cash advance to a day or two before the bill would be past due, and pay off the bill. Reason for the timing: Cash advances are charged interest from the day that they are taken. Multiple credit cards come in handy if you want to go the limit of allowable cash advances on each without having to use your card to purchase merchandise at high rates.

No one, of course, should buy on credit unless he has the income stream to pay the charges. A rule of thumb that banks use in deciding to grant credit is that a person's aggregate indebtedness, excluding home mortgage, should not exceed 20% of pre-tax income.

If you have gotten in over your head, it may be best to take out a consumer loan to pay off a number of credit-card bills. Although the consumer loan rate will not be much cheaper than the credit-card cash advanced rate, it will be significantly cheaper than the card's basic interest rate on merchandise purchases. In addition since bank credit-card payments are based on a 24-month term, one big advantage to consolidating such debt with a 36-month loan is lower monthly payments.

Source: Edward Mendlowitz, a partner with Siegel, Mendlowitz & Rich, CPAs, 310 Madison Ave., New York 10017.

ADVANTAGES OF CREDIT-CARD PURCHASES

Paying an auto mechanic by credit card is one protection against sloppy or unnecessary work. Ultimate payment can be withheld when the credit-card bill arrives. Hitches: The mechanic must be in the consumer's home state, and the bill must exceed $50. Procedure: Send letters to the credit-card company and the mechanic explaining why the repair was unsatisfactory. Propose a sum that would settle the dispute.

More information: Write for *Credit Cards: Auto Repair Protection,* Consumer Information, Dept. 636K, Pueblo, CO 81009.

• Pay for mail-order purchases with a credit card, rather than with a personal check. Reason: If you don't receive the merchandise or it's not what you expected, you can refuse to pay (under the Fair Credit Billing Act) until the matter is resolved. But if you've paid by check and the mail-order company cashes it, you may have trouble getting a refund.

Source: *Good Housekeeping.*

• Simple expense recording. With every purchase made with your credit card, write down who and why on the slip when you sign it. This enables you to keep track of your business tax deductions and expenses in a single step.

HOW TO FIND DOLLARS YOU DIDN'T KNOW YOU HAD

Few people take full advantage of the capital at their disposal. In most cases, the primary reason is that they simply don't realize the opportunities they are passing by. There are a myriad of simple ways to optimize one's resources. Consider the following:

Convert passbook savings accounts, savings bonds, etc. into better investments. Shocking: Americans still have $300 billion sitting in low-interest passbook savings accounts when they could be so easily transferred to CDs at a much better yield! Review your portfolio now, particularly bonds that have recently registered nice gains. Should you still be owning what you do? People often hold investment long after they've forgotten why they originally made them.

Borrow on life insurance. Many folks who bought life insurance back in the 1960s and 1970s (term insurance is more prevalent today) could borrow back the money at 3%–6% and reinvest it in insured CDs at a possibly higher rate.

Pay real estate taxes directly instead of through the bank. Most banks withhold an amount on monthly mortgage payments for paying the homeowner's real estate taxes. Yet in most towns, real estate tax bills are sent annually. The bank is earning interest on your money. Caution: People who elect to pay the taxes themselves must make the payments on time. Banks can call in your mortgage if the taxes are delinquent, and they'd just love to do it if you are fortunate enough to have a low-interest mortgage.

Prepay mortgage principal. People who begin repaying principal immediately along with interest can reap enormous savings. Example: Making a monthly $25 repayment of principal from day one on a $75,000, 30-year, 13% mortgage would save $59,372, and the mortgage would be paid off in 23 years and four months. (Most mortgages do allow prepayment.)

Eliminate excessive federal withholding tax. Seventy-three percent of Americans await federal tax refunds annually. In other words, they have involuntarily lent money to the government interest free. A better way: Review the W-4 form filed with your company. Estimate your deductions for the year, and increase your withholding allowances so that you will owe the IRS only a very small amount next April 15. You can claim additional witholding allowances for tax-deductible items such as job-related moving expenses, estimated losses from business or the sale of investments, and IRA contributions if you qualify for deductions under the new tax rules.

Conduct a garage sale. Turn unwanted items into cash. (Sotheby's or another auction house will appraise a possible collectible free.)

Source: William E. Donoghue, publisher of several investment newsletters, including *Donoghue's Moneyletter, Box 540, Holliston, MA 01746.*

MARGIN ACCOUNTS: WHY, WHEN AND WHY NOT

Margin accounts can be extremely advantageous when the stock market is on the way up. But when the reverse happens, you should be prepared for a call from your broker to come up with additional funds. Margin calls ("maintenance calls") are designed to protect the brokerage house against losses when the equity in the account drops below 25%–30% of the portfolio's purchase value.

At that point, you must decide whether to add more cash to the account or to sell a good portion of the securities. If you can't meet your maintenance call with cash, the brokerage firm can automatically sell all your margined shares. However, you can also instruct it to sell part of your position—but not merely enough shares to meet the shortfall in your equity. Reason: The brokerage firm doesn't want you to sell just enough to cover, since it may have to call you back every few days if the stock continues to fall. By law, you must sell three and one-third times more stock than the shortfall in your equity.

Not everyone qualifies for a margin account, nor are all margin accounts equal. It is up to the individual brokerage firm to evaluate the client and determine how much he can buy on margin, or even to refuse the margin account. These decisions do not entail a credit check—it is a gut feeling between the broker and his client. By federal law, customers must have at least $2,000 in an account before they can buy on margin.

Some brokerage houses discourage margin accounts altogether, since they can be a source of negative feelings in clients. After all it is possible for such an investor to lose more money than he initially puts up. Even investors who claim to understand that they may have to take big losses often become quite disgruntled.

Margin buying is really for sophisticated investors who like to speculate with aggressive, volatile stocks. It is not appropriate for investors who are looking for long-term value. Investors should speculate on margin only with money they can afford to lose.

Source: Louis Ehrenkrantz, director of Ehrenkrantz & King, a division of Reich & Co., 50 Broadway, New York 10004.

WHEN TO SUE YOUR STOCKBROKER

A stockbroker, like a doctor, lawyer, accountant or other professional, has a legal obligation to act in your best interests. Unfortunately, it's in your broker's best interest, but not necessarily in yours, to buy and sell as much as possible in order to generate the most commissions. If your broker is churning your account or otherwise mishandling it, you may have grounds for legal action.

Why the churning epidemic: Churning used to be the province of diresputable "boiler-room" operations: A group of salespeople shared a low-rent space and used high-pressure phone tactics to fleece clients. But people who went to big, reputable companies assumed, usually correctly, that they'd be dealt with ethically. This is no longer the case.

How to know it's happening: The typical churning victim is an unsophisticated investor, often a retired person. He is high-pressured by a broker to speculate with his bonds and blue chips with the promise that

his income will be increased substantially without any risk.

Besides the obvious new load of confirmation slips each week and monthly statement showing a high number of trades, there are other churning tipoffs. . .

• *You find a lot of interest charges on your monthly statement.* Clients often mistake interest charges for income. A common thread running through churning cases is interest charges on margin, which is actually a loan from the brokerage house to the customer at high interest rates, generally for the purpose of purchasing securities. The brokerage firm makes a profit on the interest rate.

• *Commissions charged are more than 10% of your porfolio's value in any given month.* This is especially true in a discretionary (broker-directed) account but also applies to a nondiscretionary (customer-directed) account.

• *You get margin-maintenance calls.* By law, if equity in the account falls to a specified level, the brokerage must ask you by telegram or letter to put up extra money. Otherwise, they'll sell securities in the account. Clients often have no idea what these calls are about. When they ask their broker, he fast-talks them, saying it was an error and to pay no attention to call; but he finds some other pretext to get the needed money into the account.

• *Your equity has fallen precipitously in a short time.* Some account statements seem purposely designed to mislead. Often the client assumes equity is represented by the market-value box. This figure is high because it includes whatever has been lent to the account on margin.

Other abuses: Outside of outright theft, which does happen, churning is the worst offense. However, other abuses my be ripe for legal action if they're blatant or repetitious or cause heavy losses.

Most common are problems such as the broker's failing to call you. He may not execute the transaction you wanted, and the price may change, causing you to lose, or fail to make, money. Or through ignorance or misunderstanding, a broker may make bad investments or give bad advice. Incompetence is actionable only in case of gross errors. Since you are relying on your broker's judgment, you can't sue for poor judgment. Sufficiently outrageous: A broker put a client into tax shelters that generated losses five times her income:

What to do:

• Read—and understand—your monthly statements. And don't sign anything you haven't read and understood. Educate yourself. Read about investing. Also: By law, you should get a copy of everything you sign. If you don't—ask.

• Take immediate action if you're suspicious. However, if you do have a complaint and all the transactions were in your monthly statement, which you ignored, that ostrich-like stance will give the broker the opportunity to claim that your lack of protest constituted tacit agreement. *If you have questions, go to another broker.* He'll be eager for your business and will help spot irregularities.

• Complain in writing. Send the letter by certified mail, return receipt requested. Be sure to keep a copy.

Legal remedies: You can either sue or submit your case to an arbitration panel sponsored by the securities industry. Overall, results tend to be faster and better in federal court, where the statutes under which you sue work for you. The arbitration panel includes members of the brokerage community, who are unlikely to be as sympathetic as a jury of your peers. Also, although punitive damages are not awarded under arbitration, big ones have been made by courts when the broker's behavior was atrocious.

You can sue for: Lost equity, commissions, margin interest charged, securities sold as a result of margin maintenance calls, and lost value of dividend income you might have received if the portfolio had been well tended. With a churning claim, state law allows punitive damages to be claimed for fraud.

If you have a clear-cut case, some securities lawyers will take a discounted fee against a contingency. This means you pay a lawyer a portion of his hourly rate with the agreement that he'll take the rest out of what he recovers. Important: Hire a lawyer experienced in such cases.* Sometimes a letter from an experienced securities lawyer can bring a settlement offer—especially if the case is strong and the brokerage house has tangled with him before.

*Ways to find an experienced lawyer: Ask your local bar association. Pick a name from newspaper articles about similar cases. Ask your own attorney for a reference. Ask the court clerk in your local court to show you the public records of securities cases.

Source: Attorney Dan Brecher, a specialist in securities law with Wiener, Zuckerbrot, Weiss & Brecher, 260 Madison Ave., New York, 10016.

INS AND OUTS OF ZERO COUPON BONDS

One of the hottest new investment concepts marketed to the public over the past few years is the zero coupon bond. These bonds sell under a variety of names (CATs, TIGRs, etc.). They are available in several versions—corporates, Treasuries and municipals.

They all sell at a very large discount from face value and are redeemed at maturity for face value, essentially paying accumulated compounded interest in one lump sum. If they're redeemed before maturity, the accrued interest is reflected in the price.

Why is there such a ravenous appetite for zero coupon bonds? They're cheap. . .tailored to be sold in denominations as low as $65. One can buy for $2,000 a bond that will ultimately be worth $40,000. That means they are perfectly priced for individuals who have small amounts of money they are willing to put away for 15–25 years. Obviously, the $2,000-denomination zeros are custom-tailored for IRA contributions.

Another plus: Since the interest is not paid until maturity, investors don't have to clip coupons every six months—and then figure out how to reinvest the interest payments at a good rate over a long period of time while rates go up and down. Instead, each payment is automatically accrued at the same rate.

Although the lure is the low price, zero coupon bonds are not for everyone. They certainly are not for people who might need to raise cash suddenly and be forced to bail out of the investment. Reason: Zero coupon bonds are considerably more volatile than regular bonds. If interest rates rise a great deal, a person who had to cash them in before maturity could lose a substantial amount.

Example: Should interest rates rise 3% next year, a 10-year zero coupon bond would lose 12.4% of its value within a year, while a regular bond would go down only half a percentage point.

Bottom line: These are not trading vehicles, except for the most speculative investors. Zero coupon bonds, whether taxable or tax free, are suitable for investors who are building a nest egg for a predictable expense down the road.

Tax problems: Zero coupon bonds can be a trap for many investors if they are held as taxable investments rather than in IRAs or other trust accounts. The problem: Bondholders must pay the taxes on the interest each year, even though this is essentially phantom interest. The tax burden increases each year as the interest rates grow on the compounded value.

Investors who appreciate the low pricing on zeros and don't need current income should look into purchasing tax free municipal zero coupon bonds. They are available in many denominations and maturities from a great variety of localities.

Snag: There may be some state tax on an out-of-state municipal. For instance, a New York taxpayer might have to pay state taxes on Virginia Housing Authority bonds. However, there are enough issues for most people to find local ones.

Source: Thomas Taylor, vice president, E.F. Hutton, 7 Hanover Square, New York 10027.

SHREWD OPTION PLAYS

Many investors perceive the new options instruments (such as options on the Standard & Poor's index, the telephone companies index or the gaming stock index) as being highly speculative. Although options do appeal to a particularly speculative segment of the investment public, they can also be a way for investors to conserve most of their cash, risking only a small portion of their investment capital.

Risk factor: Statistically, it has been found that 60%–70% of all options expire worthless. The price of an index or stock doesn't rise or fall enough for the option to be exercised. That means a total loss of the option investment. However, this does not make the odds as negative as they seem at first glance.

Example: You buy five options, each costing $300. Your total risk is $1,500. But if you are right even once, that single $300 option could earn you $1,500. You break even. And if you are right two out of five times, you can make a lot of money.

An investor who has a $100,000 investment portfolio might put $90,000 of it into tax-exempt municipals, which are paying about 10%. The rest could go into options. Thus the most the individual can lose of his entire capital is $10,000. But even if he loses every cent of his option money, he still winds up with $99,000 at the end of the year because of the interest on his $90,000. And if he loses all his option plays, the IRS is his partner, giving him various tax write-offs on his $10,000 loss. He gets a useful tax deduction, and his total loss is considerably less than the $1,000 ($100,000 minus $99,000).

A more optimistic example: If the investor is somewhat more judicious in his choice of options, and just 20% of his options are winners, the picture improves considerably. He has $90,000 invested tax-free. Of the $10,000 he puts into options, 20% ($2,000) turns into $6,000. The remaining $8,000 he paid for the options is lost. That means the investor had made $9,000 on his municipals and another $6,000 on his options, an end-of-the-year total of $105,000. However, the investor has also lost $8,000 on his options, which he can use as a tax loss against other earnings. Bottom line: With only $1,000 at risk (the maximum the investor could lose if all his options are duds), the investor can make a total profit of $5,000 plus the benefit of tax losses.

The investor must do better than profit 20% of the time or use options that may quadruple or quintuple his money, if he is to top a 100% investment in municipal bonds. If he is right only 30%–40% of the time, he may make an exciting profit. Or if he chooses the right option more frequently, he may do well with options that yield one and one-half to one. And he will probably do considerably better after taxes than if he has a 20% gain in the stock market. Risk comparison: An investor who puts all his money into stocks is risking everything.

Best bet: For sophisticated options usage, find a broker who understands them very well and can guide you into using them advantageously.

Source: A very savvy veteran broker at one of New York's largest brokerage houses.

WHEN TO GO FOR GOLD

There are three junctions during a typical economic cycle when gold presents a glowing buying opportunity:

• *Phase 1:* Late in the recession, when interest rates fall and the money supply growth picks up. Then there are big rallies in most investment vehicles, including gold. Reason: More people hold gold when interest rates fall and liquidity is being added, portending higher inflation down the road. That happened during the summer of 1982. Over the next year gold rose from about $300 to over $400.

• *Phase 2:* The fifth or sixth quarter of a recovery. Reason: At this point the US dollar weakens against other major currencies, and gold prices rise to reflect this weakness. The decline in the dollar at this stage of the expansion reflects the shifting growth from the US to other industrialized countries. When this happens, the US economy sucks in less capital from abroad, and the dollar declines. Key: Americans judge the value of gold in dollars. But one must determine how much of the relative weakness in gold is determined by its inherent weakness and how much by the strength of the dollar. Conclusion: The apparent low level of gold prices is due much more to the strength of the dollar than to the weakness of the gold market. So if the dollar begins to fall then the gold price in dollars will rise.

• *Phase 3:* Four to six month before industrial capacity utilization reaches 85%. At that point, the precious-metals markets begin to discount any cyclical increase in the inflation rate.

Source: Ray Dalio, president, Bridgewater Associates, an economic forecasting firm specializing in currencies and precious metals, 274 Ridgefield Rd., Wilton, CT 06897.

• Gold has been accepted as an excellent inflation hedge. Essentially, gold *does* rise with inflation, but it may underperform inflation if bought at the wrong time. Example: Gold lost 17% in price in 1983, while inflation rose 3.5%—a very poor inflation hedge. Lesson: History shows that gold offers a superior return when inflation starts rising after a long decline. But it should be sold when inflation begins to decline.

Source: *Dag Investment Letter,* 65 Lake Front Dr., Akron, OH 44319.

Taxes

WHAT SHELTER SALESMEN DON'T TELL YOU

The misconceptions, economics and tax ramifications of the shelters that the salespeople "forget" to mention are eye opening. The following two misconceptions have trapped even the most sophisticated. Beware:

Misconception #1. Tax shelters save taxes! Spend fifteen minutes with any tax shelter person and you are likely to hear, at least 50 times, that their deal will save you tax. What he doesn't say, or perhaps doesn't realize, is that tax shelters generally do not save taxes; they usually defer the time the tax is to be paid. Very few kinds of shelters actually save taxes. In fact, an uninformed decision to buy a tax shelter could actually make you pay more instead of less tax.

Misconception #2. Tax shelters are good investments! The same tax shelter salespeople who told you that tax shelters save taxes will also tell you, whether you ask or not, that their deal is also an excellent investment. In reality, most tax shelters, especially if they are promoted as tax shelters, are not good investments. Look for investment opportunities which are structured with some tax reduction and/or deferral features.

Source: *Tax Shelters: Shrewd Insights,* by Randy Bruce Blaustein, Boardroom Books, Millburn, NJ 07041.

TRAPS IN REAL ESTATE SHELTERS

The biggest mistake people make in shelter investing is buying into deals they don't understand. The key to a valid tax shelter is economic substance, the shelter's value as an investment. If you don't understand how the deal works, you can't judge its investment merit. Don't buy into a shelter unless it makes sense economically, apart from the tax benefits.

Shelter salespeople will first tell you what the tax write-offs are and then what the projected cash flow is expected to be. All this is based on certain assumptions. You can test many of them yourself. Are the assumptions logical? Do some checking.

Let's say the projections are based on an apartment house being rented 100% of the time. How likely is this to happen? A 95% occupancy rate in a low-vacancy area is optimistic. That leaves a 5% difference between the assumption and reality. That 5% comes off the projected cash flow, diminishing the return on your investment. It may mean that instead of a 10% return, you'll get only 6% or 7%. This might be enough to turn you against the shelter. Question: If something so basic to the return as the occupancy rate is inflated, what else in the offering is puffed up?

Rental-income projections may also be inflated. In a decent area in New York City, for example, office space rents for $25–$30 a square foot. If you were to see projections based on rent at $50 a foot for New York, you should be very concerned. To find out a reasonable rent projection for a given area, check with real estate brokers.

Every dollar the shelter's management company takes out in fees is a dollar less to be distributed to the limited partners. In addition to fees for continuing to manage the property, the management company may get fees for selling the property at the end. It may also get a piece of the profit on final sale. Areas of concern:

• Are the fees reasonable? Continuing management fees should not be more than

5%–6% of gross rents.

• Does the total amount that the managers get from the project seem "fair"? This is something you must decide for yourself—at what point does the managers' return affect your opinion of the whole deal?

• Do the managers get most of their fees up front? Better: Managers ride along with the investors and get their fees as they go along. That gives them a continuing stake in the property.

• Are the managing partners getting too big a share of the profit on sale? Has too large a fee been built into the selling price?

Understand the full impact of the depreciation method the shelter uses. Is it straight-line depreciation or accelerated depreciation? For short-term investors accelerated depreciation can be a problem. When you sell, all or part of your gain (depending on the type of property) will be taxed as ordinary income. Worse: Because the whole gain is brought into one tax year, you can wind up with what is called a "negative basis."

To avoid problems for short-term investors, many shelters today are using straight-line depreciation rather than accelerated depreciation.

The same tax shelter can have different consequences for different people. Individual investors should consider:

• Cash needs. Don't depend on an investment in a real estate shelter for ready cash. It's difficult to get out of any tax shelter quickly, unless you buy the whole thing. If you own only a small piece of a shelter, you're at the mercy of the general managers. They decide when you can get out.

• Deduction limits. Know the tax status of any interest costs before you buy into a shelter. If you have little or no investment income, you may run up against the deduction limit for investment interest. The amount of investment interest you can deduct each year is limited to the amount of your investment income.

• Alternative minimum tax (AMT). Tax shelter deductions, such as accelerated depreciation, may subject you to the AMT. If you land in an AMT situation, your tax shelter investment can backfire, actually increasing your tax. To be on the safe side, you should consult your tax adviser about possible AMT liability before you invest in a shelter.

In spite of the IRS crackdown on fraudulent shelters, there are still plenty of questionable deals on the market. The biggest trap is inflated valuation. The tax benefits of the shelter are based on the value placed on the property. Disreputable promoters sometimes assign inflated values to a shelter's assets to increase the tax benefits. Trap: The IRS can disallow depreciation deductions to the extent that the "price" of the property exceeds its fair market value. This can result in penalties for understating tax.

Real estate shelters provide solid tax benefits but not terribly dramatic ones. They must be carefully evaluated to be sure they make sense as investment vehicles aside from their tax aspects.

Source: Herbert C. Speiser, partner in the international accounting firm Touche Ross & Co., 1633 Broadway, New York 10019.

FIND ALL YOUR TAX BREAKS

Here are five excellent sources to consult when you're searching for deductions and credits and big tax-saving opportunities. (Remember, the IRS isn't going to tell you about a tax break you may have overlooked. That's your job.)

1. Your checkbook register. Identify anything that looks remotely tax deductible. Then research the idea. Obvious: Checks to doctors, dentists and charities. . .checks for business expenses and trips.

2. Credit card statements. Use the same method as with your checkbook register.

3. The long-form 1040. Carefully review last year's long form, line by line, for anything that might apply to you for the first time. Look at Schedule A for itemized deductions, form 2106 for employee business expenses and form 3903 for moving expenses. Also glance through your tax returns for the past two years to make sure you're not overlooking items you claimed previously.

4. A tax professional. Even if you are comfortable handling your own taxes—and everyone should take an active role in this very important part of his finances—you should have an expert check to see that you haven't been cheating yourself out of legitimate tax breaks. Recommended: Consult a tax professional at least once every three years.

5. Specialized newspapers, magazines and newsletters. . . prime sources for tax information. It's your responsibility to keep your eyes open for tax savings.

Taxpayers consistently miss out on tax breaks, losing billions of dollars each year. The most commonly overlooked tax savings:

• Unreimbursed employee business expenses and "miscellaneous" expenses are deductible to the extent they exceed 2% of your adjusted gross income. Despite this limit, you may still have some deductible expenses. Look for expenses your employer would not pay for, such as a new office desk set and lamp, extra business driving, cab fares to meetings and seminars, long-distance business calls made from your home telephone, business gifts (up to $25 per recipient), a new briefcase or calculator.

• In totaling your miscellaneous expenses look for investment advice and other expenses associated with your portfolio. Include: Investment advisory services, travel away from home to look after investment property, safe-deposit-box rent, cab fare to consult with your broker, telephone calls, investment books and periodicals.

• Job-hunting expenses. The cost of looking for a new job in your current trade or business is deductible whether or not you land the job. Included: Employment agency fees, career counseling, expenses of preparing, typing, printing and mailing resumes and cover letters, transportation costs and telephone calls, the cost of advertising for a new job and the cost of business publications and newspapers you buy for the want ads.

• Business expenses associated with a trip where you tacked on a personal vacation. You must, however, be able to show that the primary purpose of the trip was business.

Source: Paul N. Strassels, former IRS tax-law specialist and publisher of *The Washington Money Letter*, Box 14151, Washington, DC 20044.

DEDUCTIBLE MEDICAL EXPENSES

• Medical transportation. A taxpayer's dependent adult son had an operation in an out-of-state clinic. The parent flew to the clinic each day during the postoperative period. IRS ruling: The parent's airplane fare was a deductible medical expense. So was the cost of renting a car to drive to the clinic and hospital. Key: The clinic required someone to attend to patients during their postoperative period.
Letter Ruling 8321042.

• Parents who drove their disabled son to an out-of-state clinic for treatment could deduct travel costs plus expenses for meals and lodging on the trip.
William L. Pfersching, TC Memo 1983-341.

• A patient with emphysema and bronchitis was advised by his doctor to exercise by swimming. Because local pool hours didn't coincide with his work schedule, he built his own indoor pool. He deducted the cost of fuel, electricity, insurance and other maintenance expenses. IRS position: The existence of a diving board and the lack of medical equipment showed that the pool was for nondeductible personal use. Tax Court: Expenses were deductible. The patient's need to exercise his lungs didn't require any medical equipment except the pool. Recreational use by his family was incidental.
Herbert Cherry, TC Memo 1983-470.

• Deductible wig. A doctor prescribed a wig to relieve the mental distress of a person whose hair fell out. The cost of the wig was a deductible medical expense.
Source: *Revenue Ruling 62-189.*

• The cost of electrolysis qualifies as a deductible medical expense.
Source: *Letter Ruling 8442018.*

• Deductible diet and exercise. A taxpayer who suffered from high blood pressure could deduct the cost of a diet and exercise program prescribed by his doctor as treatment for the condition.
Letter Ruling 8251045.

• Personal injury. An individual who wins a personal-injury lawsuit gets a double tax break. First, the damage award is tax free. Second, his medical expenses are deductible, even if he pays them out of the award.
Kelly B. Niles, CA-9, No. 82-4278.

THE CREDIT-CARD BREAK

There's an exception to the general rule that you can take a tax deduction only in the year you pay for a deductible expense.

For tax-purposes, payment made by credit card is considered to be made on the date of the transaction, not on the date you pay the credit-card issuer. You can sign for an expense this year and deduct it on this year's return, even though you don't actually pay the bill until next year.

Medical and dental expenses paid by credit card are deductible in the year the charge is made (*Revenue Ruling* 78-39).

Sales tax on items you buy with a credit card before the end of the year is deductible the year you purchase the items.

Charitable contributions made by credit card are also deductible in the year the charge is made. (*Revenue Ruling* 78-38).

THE TIME FOR GIVING

The end of the year is the time for giving, and generosity carries tax rewards. Smart giving:
• To reap the greatest tax advantage for contributions to charity, give long-term securities that have gone up in value since you bought them. You get a deduction for the full fair market value of the securities (not the cost), and the built-in long-term gain is not taxed to you. *TRAP:* The gain will be taxed if you should happen to be subject to the alternative minimum tax (AMT). See your tax adviser. A large gift of appreciated money may itself put you into the AMT.
• Don't donate loss property to charity. Sell the property, deduct the loss on your tax return, and contribute the proceeds.
• If you give artwork or collectibles to charity, make sure the property is used for the charity's main activity or purpose. If it isn't, your deduction is limited.
• Gifts of clothing and household items are deductible at their current value. But you'll need full information, including an inventory listing the items contributed and their value, in order to satisfy the IRS.
• Gifts to family members are encouraged by our tax laws. You can give an unlimited amount of property to your spouse completely free of federal gift tax. And you can give other family members up to $10,000 per recipient, per year, without incurring any gift tax. You can double that $10,000 if you and your spouse jointly make the gift to each recipient.
• For long-range income tax planning, you can use gifts to family members and others to shift taxable income to those in lower tax-brackets.

SMART GIVING

Start the year right by planning to use your annual gift-tax exclusion of $10,000 per donee ($20,000 per donee if your spouse consents to joint gifts). The exclusion is not cumulative. It's wasted each year you don't use it. To make gifts without worsening your income or cash flow: Borrow from the bank to make the gift. Give a policy of cash-value insurance on your own life. Forgive a loan that you never intended to inforce. Transfer securities that aren't currently paying anything but which have some present value. Give jewelry to your grandchildren.
• A son paid his mother's medical expenses

with money he withdrew from her bank account under a power of attorney. The IRS disallowed the son's deduction for these expenses, saying the money was really the mother's. But the Court of Appeals allowed the deduction. The money was legally his— a gift from his mother to him.

John M. Rich, CA-5, 82-4463.

DEDUCTIONS FOR MANAGING YOUR MONEY

• IRA fees are tax deductible. The IRS has ruled that fees paid to the trustee of an individual retirement account are deductible. Also, the fees do not count toward the annual $2,000 limit in IRA contributions.
Letter Ruling 8329049.

• Management fees for bank money-market accounts are a deductible investment expense. The fees are not for the privilege of writing checks (nondeductible) but for maintaining an interest-bearing account.
Letter Ruling 8345067.

• Investor's expenses. An individual invested in stocks, savings accounts and property located in a distant state. He claimed business-expense deductions for the cost of travel, auto depreciation and maintaining an office at home. But the IRS disallowed the deductions. Tax Court: For the IRS. Investing to collect income in the form of dividends and interest is not a business and will not support business-expense deductions.
C. Fredrick Frick, TC Memo 1983-733.

COMPENSATION LOOPHOLE

Employee business expenses, along with the cost of investment advice, tax preparation fees and other miscellaneous items (such as the cost of subscribing to business or investment publications) are deductible, under tax reform, only to the extent that their total *exceeds* 2% of adjusted gross income. Thus a person with adjusted gross income of $50,000 can get *no* deduction for the first $1,000 worth of such items.

When executives have large unreimbursed business expenses, they may do better by negotiating with their employers for an increase in their reimbursements instead of a raise. *Contrast:* If the executive gets a raise, it will be taxed, while the executive will lose at least part of the deduction for the unreimbursed expenses. On the other hand, an increase in reimbursements will be tax free and completely cover the cost of expenses.

WHAT ARE THE CHANCES OF AN AUDIT

• Contrary to the tough-guy image the IRS likes to project, it audits only a small percentage of tax returns each year.

Taxpayers in upper-income brackets have a greater than average chance of being audited. In 1983, 4.9% of taxpayers making $50,000 or more were audited. The percentage of upper-income audits is more than three times greater than that of other taxpayers.
IRS Commissioner's Annual Report.

• Don't be fooled by statistics showing a low possibility of audit. The overall possibility may be low, but many factors can increase it significantly: High income (the higher the income, the more likely an audit). Above-average tax deductions. Returns prepared by anyone on the "problem preparer" list. Unanswered questions. Sloppy returns. Statements about constitutional rights. Failure to report interest or dividends (the IRS's matching programs are getting better). And although the number of audits is still low, the average tax assessment is increasing.

THE IRS's HIT LIST

First: Illegal tax protest. The IRS will go after a tax protestor for as little as $25 in unpaid taxes, just to set an example. Anyone who refuses to file a completed return, arguing against the constitutionality of taxes or the way the country is being run, will be labeled a tax protester and be charged a $500 penalty for filing a frivolous return, plus other penalties and interest for unpaid taxes.

Second: Abusive tax shelters: The IRS is looking for large loss items usually under charitable contributions on Schedule A, partnerships on Schedule E and investment losses on Schedule D.

Third: Unreported income. The IRS estimates that most of its tax collection problems stem from nonreported income rather than excessive deductions. Make sure you properly report all your dividends, interest, profits and losses from securities transactions, and, of course, wages on your return. The IRS is checking what you report against who the people who pay you report.

Source: Paul N. Strassels, a former IRS tax-law specialist, publishes the *Washington Money Letter,* Box 14151, Washington, DC 20044.

AUDIT ANGLES

Audits are not entirely a matter of chance. While there's no way to eliminate the danger of an audit, you can reduce the risk. The simple steps:

• Get extensions and file at the last minute. . . in the fall. An automatic four-month extension, plus the extra two months you usually get if a second extension is granted, advances your filing date to October 15.

People who file in the fall are less likely to be audited than those who file by April 15. Reason: Most targeted returns are selected during the summer months. By fall, most of the year's quota of returns to be audited has been filled. Caution: Filing extensions do not extend the time for paying tax. If you don't pay at least 90% of the tax you expect to owe by April 15, you'll be hit with a penalty and possible loss of the extension.

• Attach detailed infomation and substan-

tiation to your return, if you have an unusual or complicated transaction that IRS computers will automatically question. After the computer has selected your return for possible audit, an IRS employee looks it over. You may be able to ward off an audit by explaining the transaction to that person. Caution: Do not mail originals, send copies only.

Send in full documentation for unusually large deductions, such as large casualty losses. Attach copies of appraisals for substantial charitable donations of property.

• Answer all questions on the return, including those that don't apply to you. If you don't have a bank account in a foreign country say so. Don't skip the item. IRS computers automatically flag questions that go unanswered.

• Fill in the return carefully. A sloppy return indicates a careless taxpayer. The IRS may examine the return to see if carelessness led to mistakes.

If your return is selected for audit you'll get a notification letter. The items the IRS is interested in are checked off or written in on that letter. How to proceed then:

• Avoid repetitive audits. The *Internal Revenue Manual* says that taxpayers shall not be subjected to needless and repetitive examinations. If you are being audited on items that were examined in either of the two preceding years, and that audit produced no change (or only a small change) in your tax bill, you can request that you not be audited again for the same items. Tell the auditor that you qualify under the repetitive audit provisions of the *Manual.* Send the auditor (1) a copy of the prior year's appointment letter showing which items were chosen for the audit, (2) a copy of the no-change letter, and (3) a copy of the prior year's tax return.

• Try to resolve the issue by mail. If only a few items have been chosen for audit and you can substantiate them, mail in copies of your proof with a covering letter at least ten days before your scheduled appointment. Give a telephone number where you can be reached during the day should the agent have any questions. If all goes well, you'll get a letter back from the agent, though not immediately, telling you that your return has been accepted as filed—examination closed.

• Don't antagonize the agent. Be courteous and businesslike. If you can't keep an appointment, call and change it. If you missed an appointment, call as soon as possible. There may be time to reschedule.

• Be prepared to appeal if the audit results in an unfavorable report. There are formal and informal ways to get redress. If the agent has been unreasonable, overaggressive or clearly wrong about the law, insist on an immediate conference with the agent's group manager. An experienced supervisor may be able to find a way out of an impasse that isn't apparent to a newly trained agent. If you get nowhere with the group manager, you can take your case to the Appeals Division of the IRS where the hazards of litigation will be considered. That is, the chance that the government might lose in court if it litigates the case.

• Going to court can pay off, even when it seems that the law is against you. By filing a court petition, you get an extra pre-trial meeting with the IRS attorneys. You may be able to work out a better deal with the lawyers than you could with other IRS employees. Reason: They are primarily concerned with disposing of cases. A court contest costs the IRS time and money. So if there's no special reason for the IRS to litigate, you may be able to work out a favorable settlement.

The bottom line: Good record keeping is the key to winning your battle with the IRS. Be prepared to document your deductions with receipts, canceled checks and bills marked paid. The IRS follows a simple rule: If you spent it, you should be able to prove it. Without proof, you cannot fight. And without good records, you won't be able to convince the IRS to allow your deductions.

Source: Edward Mendlowitz, a partner in Siegel, Mendlowitz & Rich, CPAs, 310 Madison Ave., New York 10017.

HOW THE IRS GETS INSIDE INFORMATION

• The IRS has the power to summons whatever information may be relevant to the audit of your tax return. The most commonly summoned records are bank and brokerage firm records. But the courts have also ordered a department store to turn over to the IRS copies of a taxpayer's monthly statements. Presumably, these spending records would help the examiners determine whether the taxpayer was reporting all his income by enabling them to estimate his cash flow and the extent of his wealth.

US v. Lazarus Department Stores, DCSD, Ohio.

• The auditor can ask to see car repair bills even though you took the 21¢ per mile deduction and didn't itemize car expenses. The reason: Repair bills often show the odometer reading on the car being serviced. By comparing readings at various dates, the auditor gets an idea of how far the car has been driven.

Suppose a bill in January showed an odometer reading of 10,000 miles and a December bill showed only 20,000. A taxpayer would have a hard time claiming a deduction for 50,000 miles driven during the year.

• Some of the country's biggest data marketing firms have refused to participate in the IRS's scheme to track down cheats by matching "lifestyle" information collected by the companies with IRS taxpayer lists. The companies say the information they gather couldn't help the IRS because it can't accurately predict a taxpayer's income.

• Local federal attorneys have been given authority to seek search warrants in connection with criminal tax cases without prior approval of the Justice Department in Washington. The number of warrants is expected to rise markedly above the handful that are currently issued each year. Reason for the new policy: The dramatic rise in the number of fraudulent tax-avoidance schemes.

• The IRS was investigating a taxpayer and

ordered his bank to produce the records of his account. The bank refused because it was a joint account, and the IRS hadn't sent notice to the account's co-owner. The District Court ruled for the bank, and the IRS appealed. Court of Appeals: There's no requirement that the account's co-owner be warned of the disclosure. Produce the records.

First Bank, CA-2, No. 83-6350.

• Accountant-client privilege does not exist. That's what the Supreme Court held while ordering a private accounting firm to turn over to the IRS its confidential assessment of a taxpayer's tax strategies.

US v. Arthur Young & Co., S.Ct., No. 82-687.

• Informant danger. If a trusted friend, or relative or employer turns on you, steals your personal financial records and delivers them to the IRS, there's nothing you can do to keep the IRS from using them against you. Key: The IRS didn't take the records from you illegally, the person you trusted did.

Resmondo vs. US, DCSD Fla, No. 79-8166.

• Pressure is on Caribbean tax havens to provide the IRS with criminal and civil tax information. The bait: Liberal rules will permit business expense deductions for people attending conventions in Caribbean countries that cooperate. Eligible islands include: Anguilla, The Bahamas, Barbados, Cayman Islands, Grenada, Netherlands Antilles, British Virgin Islands.

Interest and Dividend Tax Compliance Act.

MANAGERIAL ATTITUDES

• Middle managers face more job related stress than either higher-ups or subordinates. Problems: Heavy responsibilities without proportional compensation. Long hours. Nagging work concerns that can't be left at the office. Extensive travel. Frequent transfers that place strain on the family.

Source: *Workrights* by Robert Ellis Smith, E.P. Dutton, Inc., 2 Park Ave., New York 10016.

• Senior managers believe that someone promoted into their own position would need 18 months, on the average, to learn the job. Their immediate subordinates, however, feel that they could learn the senior positions in about five or six months.

Source: *Competence and Power in Managerial Decision Making* by F. Heller and B. Wilpert, John Wiley & Sons, 605 Third Ave., New York 10158.

• Female bosses help their subordinates get more raises and promotions than do male bosses, according to a study. Reason: The "female" style of management shows more concern for employees and office relationships. And women bosses were found more open to new ideas. Result: Higher office productivity and more upward mobility.

Source: Research by Carl Camden, Ph.D., Cleveland State University, quoted in *Self.*

TIPS FOR A SUCCESSFUL MANAGER

• Creative procrastination. If you feel like putting off an unpleasant task, turn to another job related to your overall goal. Example: If you're procrastinating on some correspondence, you might address the envelopes and gather the backup material you'll need to write the letters. Bottom line: By varying the sequence of tasks, you may get the job done in the same (or even less) time.

Source: *Creative Time Management* by J.L. Barkas, Prentice-Hall, Englewood Cliffs, NJ 07632.

• You can fight procrastination by "giving in" to it for 15 minutes. Example: Stare at the paperwork on your desk, but forbid yourself to touch it. After 15 minutes of growing uneasiness, you'll be chomping at the bit to get at those papers.

Source: *The Organized Executive* by Stephanie Winston, Warner Books, 666 Fifth Ave., New York 10103.

• Body language. When entering an office, pause slightly at the door and again in front of the desk. The more time you take, the more status the other person attributes to you.

Source: Debra A. Benton, managing partner of Benton Management Resources, 90 Corona St., Denver 80218, and teacher of charisma classes.

• To catch up with your desk after a trip or illness, first clear it completely. Sort everything (without reading) into four boxes: High priority, routine, magazines and ad mail. Then start at the top of the high-priority pile, disposing of one item at a time, before moving to the other boxes. Suggestion: Stop all incoming calls and visitors for one day. If you can't finish in a day, set aside one or two hours each morning until done.

Source: *Execu-Time*, Box 631, Lake Forest, IL 60045.

• Process every paper as it comes across your desk. Putting "lower priority" papers aside can be costly, both in time and in missed opportunities. Stick to TRAF: Toss it, refer it, act on it or file it.

Source: *The Organized Executive*, by Stephanie Winston, Warner Books, 666 Fifth Ave., New York 10103.

• Constant drop-in visitors can disrupt and damage a manager's work. If a co-worker or subordinate continually abuses the privilege, don't be afraid to be a little curt or rude. You can always apologize later—and the visitor will think twice before disturbing you next time.

Source: *Execu-Time*, Box 631, Lake Forest, IL 60045.

AVOID THE MEETING TRAP

The average US manager works 10–12 hours a day and takes work home at night too. Prime culprit: Office meetings, which swallow 35%–40% of the working day. Helpful: Hold fewer meetings. Send out a highly structured agenda to all participants at least a day in advance to improve their preparation.

Source: A survey by the Goodrich & Sherwood Co., 521 Fifth Ave., New York 10017.

TO REDUCE STRESS AT YOUR DESK

Make certain that your chair is comfortable.
• Quiet your telephone's ring.
• Alter the lighting to reduce glare. . .or increase brightness.
• Personalize your work space with photos, posters, etc.
• Adopt at least a partial closed-door policy for your office. (If you have no way to be alone in your office, find a place elsewhere in the building where you can take breathers.)
• Avoid tight shirt collars. . .they can cut blood flow to the brain and result in light-headedness and panic attacks. Tightly cinched belts are troublesome, too.
• Establish a regular time for meals, especially lunch.

Source: *The Termination Trap* by Stephen Cohen, Williamson Publishing, Church Hill Rd., Charlotte, VT 05445.

TIME MANAGEMENT STRATEGIES

Start each workday with a five-minute priority-setting conference. Review plans for the day with people working with you, including secretaries. Decide together which task needs to be done first. *Key:* Always limit the session to five minutes. Don't offer conferees chairs or coffee, or you'll be faced with a staff meeting. *(Editor's note:* Frequently more effective. . .holding the meeting at the end of the previous day.)

Source: *Stress Management* by Edward A. Charlesworth, Atheneum, 597 Fifth Ave., New York 10017.

• Promise everything later than you think you can deliver it. Advantages: You'll finish ahead of schedule. Delays won't throw you. You'll work better without deadline pressure. You'll gain a reputation for reliability.

Source: *Martin's Magic Motivation Book* by Phyllis Martin, St. Martin's Press, 175 Fifth Ave., New York 10010.

• The 80/20 Principle: About 20% of what you do will give you 80% of your results. Example: 20% of your research will get you 80% of your report. Recommended: Target the "right" 20%; then do it the best you can. That will pay off better than doing everything else magnificiently.

Source: *Creative Time Management* by J.L. Barkas, Prentice-Hall, Inc., Englewood Cliffs, NJ 07632.

WHEN AND HOW TO CHANGE JOBS

It's time for you to leave the company when:
• You realize management is neglecting its basic business.
• Your company has had a sensational run for several years. (A downturn is inevitable. It's best to leave as a winner.)
• You're excluded from sharing in the company's success.
• Your firm isn't keeping up with competition.
• You've run out of interest.
• You've run out of ideas.
• You start aiming at a position a relative of management might want.
• You don't know why you're there. (Sketch out a career plan and find the job that will be your next step up.)

Source: *The Official Guide to Success* by Tom Hopkins, Warner Books, 666 Fifth Ave., New York 10103.

• Competence on the job cannot overcome

bad chemistry—a personality conflict with other executives in the company, particularly the boss. A candid, conciliatory management style, for instance, may only lose your respect in a more aggressive, conspiratorial environment. Recommended: If you can't fit in with the corporate culture, the best way to preserve your self-confidence (and your career) is to leave.

Source: Patricia O'Toole, author of *Corporate Messiah: The Hiring and Firing of Million-Dollar Managers*, William Morrow & Co., 105 Madison Ave., New York 10016.

• When voluntarily departing from a firm, speak of "mixed feelings" about leaving. Obviously, everyone knows you think you're off to something better, but soft-pedal your glee. On the other hand, it's foolish to pretend that you're not pleased and proud of the move you're making.

Source: Dr. Marilyn Machlowitz, New York-based management consultant, career counselor and lecturer.

COMMON CAREER MYTHS

• Myth #1: You must have a five-year plan. Goals are good, as long as they are not rigid. Rigid views of where you want to be (and how you get there) actually reduce options.
• Myth #2: You have to stay in your first job at least two years. There is no sense sticking it out if you are in a dead-end situation. Give it three to six months, and if it is a mistake, start looking.
• Myth #3: Your boss will take care of you. Superiors can promote your interest, but in large corporations their powers have been eroded by salary ceiling and head-count freezes. Your advancement is your responsibility.
• Beware of the "more school is better' myth. In the present economy, unless students are attending outstanding schools, a JD or MBA degree might not be worth the time, trouble and expense.

Source: Dr. Marilyn Machlowitz, a New York-based career and human resources consultant.

JOB STRATEGIES

• College graduates are generally better off accepting their first reasonable job offer, even if it falls short of salary expectations. Beginning salary is less important than a quick start in the business world. Bright, ambitious people inevitably move up.

Source: Peter Vranes, Thirty-Three Personnel Center, Chicago, quoted in *Business Week*.

• Job-hopping to get fancier titles and higher salaries may not be the best way to reach the top. A recent survey found that 76% of company chairmen or chief executive officers had been with the firm more than 10 years. Fifty percent had stayed with the same company more than 20 years.

Source: Survey by Russell Reynolds Associates, executive recruiters, 245 Park Ave., New York 10017.

THE BEST CAREER OPPORTUNITIES

• Over the next 20–30 years will be for computer technicians and legal assistants. *Next best:* Other computer-related jobs (analysts, programmers, operators). Office-machinery repairers. Physical therapists and assistants. Electrical engineers and technicians. Employment interviewers.

Source: *Occupational Outlook* by the US Department of Labor.

• Don't believe all you hear about massive job shifts from manufacturing to service industries. What's really happening: Service industries are indeed burgeoning, but they're becoming automated at such a fast pace that they're taking fewer and fewer people away from factory jobs. Increased productivity from computerization will produce more services from fewer and fewer workers. . .and middle-management jobs in service companies will be greatly automated in the near future. Fortunately, the trend won't lead to unemployment, because fewer people will be entering the labor force.

Source: Nobel laureate Wassily Leontief of New York University.

TIPS FOR JOB HUNTING

• Make a list of 20 personal contacts who can get wind of opportunities or spread word of your availability.

Research a list of 50 companies in the chosen field.

Send letters to target executives and middlemen. Then follow up with phone calls to request get-acquainted interviews. (Avoid direct job solicitations at this point. A company with no immediate openings may still be useful for referrals.) Spend about 75% of your time on this process. Shoot for at least one interview a day.

Spend the rest of your time on classified ads and recruiting firms.

Write sincere follow-up letters to nail down a referral or—when appropriate—a job.

A job campaign is a numbers game. If you broadcast your message widely enough, the law of averages will ultimately take care of you.

Source: Goodrich & Sherwood Co., an executive search firm, 521 Fifth Ave., New York 10017.

• Best job sources: Job searchers rank their success with the various avenues:

	GOOD	FAIR	POOR
Friends, colleagues	79%	9%	3%
Recruiters	18%	49%	15%
Newspaper ads	3%	15%	44%
Trade press ads	—	27%	38%

Source: A post-search survey conducted by Eaton Swain Associates, 405 Lexington Ave., New York 10174.

• Job hunters frequently figure that "more is better" when it comes to ambition. They attempt to show in interviews just how ambitious they are. Temper this. Personnel directors regard such expressions as grandiose and unrealistic. Far from helping the candidate win the job, the expression of unbridled ambition may prevent being considered for it at all.

Source: Dr. Marilyn Machlowitz, a New York-based management consultant, career counselor and lecturer.

. . . the first 10 seconds often determines the outcome of a job interview. *Behavior that leads to rejection:* A weak handshake. Poor eye contact. Slouching in the chair. Lack of enthusiasm. Sloppy grooming. Smoking. Hostility. Boastfulness. Condescension to the secretary or receptionist.

Source: Robert Half International, Inc., 522 Fifth Ave., New York 10036.

WHAT MAKES A SUCCESSFUL ENTREPRENEUR

• Entrepreneurs average 3.8 failures before a final success. What sets apart winners: Persistence. Unlike the average business-person, whose ego can be shattered by failure, the successful entrepreneur never loses a sense of self-worth.

Source: Lisa M. Amoss, professor at Tulane University's School of Business, cited in *Success!*

• Entrepreneurs fall into three basic categories: Craftspeople, who use their business as a vehicle for doing what they like to do. . . growth-focused types, who seek to achieve certain financial goals. . . and independence-oriented people, who start their own firms to avoid working for others. Not surprisingly, the growth-focused group has the greatest financial success.

Source: Study by Arnold C. Cooper, professor of management, Krannert Graduate School of Management, Purdue University, cited in *Working Woman.*

• Key to success. "When I work 14 hours a day, seven days a week, I get lucky."

Source: Dr. Armand Hammer, oil company executive, art patron and one of the wealthiest men in the world, quoted in *M.*

Family Life

ALL ABOUT MARRYING AND REMARRYING

Today, with predictions that two out of every three marriages will end in divorce, couples who are marrying need all the help they can get. Here is some advice for a good start:

Choose the right person for the right reasons. The most important thing the couple should do is to consider why they want to marry and whether they have selected the best person to meet those goals.

Too often, they have made the wrong choice—because they have needs they don't admit even to themselves. They know what they want, but even though the person they plan to marry doesn't fill the bill, they think he/she will change.

Have realistic expectations about the marriage. Another person can do only so much for you. No one person can fill every need. It is important for both partners to develop their own lives and interests and not depend solely on each other.

Learn to communicate. Get issues out on the table and talk about them. Try to reach conclusions regarding conflicts rather than letting them stay unresolved. They are right when they say, "Never go to sleep on an argument."

Respect the other person's style of communication. People express affection in different ways. Women tend to be emotional and want flowers and wine as signs of love. Men tend to be more practical and to express their caring in their actions.

Instead of expecting a spouse to react as you do, try to be sensitive to what he or she is telling you in his/her own way.

Respect the other person's feelings about space and distance. Many people have difficulty understanding someone else's needs for privacy and time alone. Some like a lot of separate space. Others want to merge constantly. Deciding what kind of distance to settle on is a major task. Important: Remember, conflicts about space needs can be resolved by trial and error—and patience.

Create a new lifestyle. Each partner comes with different concepts about customs, handling money, vacations, etc. One may be used to making a big thing about celebrating holidays and birthdays, the other not. Combine the best elements to get a richer blend that is distinctly your own.

Draw up an agenda of important issues. Many people are put off by legal contracts concerning property settlements, but consider a written list that makes you talk about how money, sex and vacations will be handled, whether or not you want children, how the household chores will be divided, etc. You don't have to agree on everything. You can agree to disagree on certain points or to explore a solution together. But at least you will have opened a dialogue on expectations, roles and beliefs, one that can be continued periodically.

Source: Barbara C. Freedman, CSW, director of the Divorce and Remarriage Counseling Center, 340 E. 52 St., New York 10022.

DANGERS TO A GOOD MARRIAGE

Living together before marriage can be a trap. Marital satisfaction tends to decline in the first decade. Since cohabiters have already been together for awhile, they may feel the strains earlier. They have already established a residence, so marriage is just a new set of responsibilities with little excitement. People who marry without having lived together feel they are carving a new mutual identity in the community.

Source: Roy E.L. Watson, PhD, University of Victoria, British Columbia, writing in *Medical Aspects of Human Sexuality*, 360 Lexington Ave., New York 10077.

• If you need more time to be by yourself, explain your feelings to your partner. (Be patient in waiting for changes.) Reserve a set time for solitude in your daily schedule. Develop outside interests. When the desire for "space" may mask a problem: You're uncomfortable when you spend time with your mate. You avoid discussing problems with each other. You're frightened by the feelings that go with intimacy.

Source: Dr. Stuart S. Asch, professor of clinical psychiatry, Cornell University Medical College, in *USA Today*

• Games people play kill relationships. Even if you "win" by entrapping your partner, you both lose in the end. Particularly dangerous: Jealousy. . .The Silent Treatment. . .Withholding Sex. . .Bargaining. . .Keeping Score. . .Getting Even. . . Complaining to Outsiders. . .Using Children. . .One-upmanship. . .Buying Love.

Source: *The Love Test* by Harold Bessell, William Morrow & Co., 105 Madison Ave., New York 10016.

WHAT EVERY GOOD PARENT SHOULD KNOW

• Family myth: An only child tends to be selfish, lonely and maladjusted. Fact: Recent studies show that the size of a family matters far less than its social and economic status—and the presence of both parents in the home. Other findings: Compared to children with siblings, only children are just as popular with peers. . .express the same degree of general happiness in their adult years. . .are just as healthy, both physically and mentally. . .score higher in intelligence tests. . .have higher academic aspirations. . .reach higher levels of education. . .and attain more prestige on the job.

Source: Research by Dr. Toni Falbo, associate professor, University of Texas at Austin.

• Unattractive children usually develop other assets that enhance their personalities. Examples: Loyalty. A capacity for initimacy. The ability to share interests and feelings. Result: They often have an edge in the quest for success and happiness over the much more attractive children who have

lived with undue emphasis on physical qualities. The most important trait: Self-assurance. The person who has this quality quickly overcomes any possible deficiencies in physical appearance.

• Behavior problems among children have often been linked to chemical additives and vitamin deficiencies. But recent studies turned up two surprising villians: Wheat and milk.

When wheat was withdrawn from their diets, some problem children behaved normally—only to revert when they ate it again.

In another study, children with behavioral disorders were found to drink more than three pints of milk a day, as compared with less than half a pint in the non-offending group. Conclusion: When milk provides most of a child's protein, it can lead to an imbalance in amino acids, which in turn affects behavior.

Source: Study by Alexander Schauss, director of the American Institute for Biosocial Research, in *New Scientist*.

• Children feel stress in the same manner as adults. Prime root of stress: Anxiety over school performance. Special problem: When a child who is naturally slower-paced is born to parents who are high achievers. They may expect too much. Other sources of stress: Insufficient playtime. . .minimal contact with the extended family (grandparents, aunts, uncles, cousins). . .peer pressure to keep up with fashions and trends. . .too much responsibility too soon. . .excessive TV watching.

• Addicts are made, not born. According to a study by the National Academy of Sciences, children are more likely to become drug or alcohol abusers if they are physically abused, lied to or humiliated, or if their parents are addicts. Other potential causes: Deprivation or overindulgence, shifts from too much to too little discipline or praise.

IMPROVING YOUR CHILD'S READING SKILLS

Reading aloud to children is a proven method of improving reading readiness and skills. It builds vocabulary and comprehension while stimulating interest, emotional development and imagination. To get the most out of reading aloud to your youngsters:

• Pick a daily time for story hour so that it becomes a tradition. (Bedtime is usual, but consider early morning.)

• Start with picture books and work up to stories and novels. Don't read above a child's emotional level. However, occasionally stretching his intellectual level can be a good challenge.

• Don't put reading in direct competition with television by asking a child to choose between them.

• Don't read a book that you don't like yourself. Children will sense your lack of enjoyment.

Source: *The Read-Aloud Handbook* by James Trelease, Penguin Books, 299 Murray Hill Pkwy., Rutherford, NJ 07073.

• Dr. Seuss was right. Preschoolers who learn to recognize rhymes become better readers later on, according to a recent study. And when low-scoring children were trained in sound recognition, their reading levels improved far more than those schooled in concepts and categories.

Source: Study at Oxford University, in *Psychology Today.*

TRAPS IN ACCELERATED EARLY LEARNING

The first three years of a child's life are the most important for future development—to school age and beyond. Result: A wave of expensive, elaborate early-learning programs. Children are rushed to swim by the age of three months, read by one year, and operate a computer at two.

Wanting your child to do better is very praiseworthy and understandable. But when you define *better* simply as *bright*, and you desperately reach out for almost any program that comes along, you're taking a great risk. Young children are heart as much as mind. Balance is the key. There's more to development than a surprising vocabulary. It's much easier to produce a bright,

facile, obnoxious child than an unspoiled, likable, decent one.

In B.L. White's view, none of these accelerated-learning programs are useful in the development of a well-rounded child. (An exception is Gymboree, a low-pressure exercise instruction program for parents and their babies.) At best, they're superfluous to the child's natural learning process. At worst, they intrude on time and the child's need to develop social skills and motor skills.

In addition, too many parents come to value their children's achievement over the children themselves. Common results: Precocious, unhappy children who are socially incompetent.

There's growing evidence, in fact, that hurrying babies and young children intellectually often backfires in the future. David Elkind of Tufts University, a leader in the field of children's learning, has found that those who learn to read by the age of three are more likely to have reading problems later on. Key: Although these children learned the mechanics of reading, they understood little of its content. (In addition, Elkind found serious stress symptoms in three- to five-year-old early learners, including headaches and stomach aches.)

The Harvard Preschool Project, studied several hundred families over a 13-year period. They defined a competent three-year-old by both intellectual *and* social criteria. These "model" children were imaginative, and they were good observers. They anticipated consequences better than the norm. They knew how to get attention in socially acceptable ways. Although they didn't hesitate to approach an adult when they needed help, they first tried to solve problems by themselves. In fantasy play, they often assumed the roles of grown-ups. They were good leaders, but they also knew how to follow.

Then the project looked at their parents Leading characteristics: As soon as the babies were ready to crawl (usually around seven months), the parents encouraged them to roam freely about the house. These children weren't penned up for long periods in playpens or jump seats. Instead, they were given full access to the living areas (which had been childproofed for safety)—to exercise their boundless curiosity, improve control over their bodies, and explore their new world.

These children didn't need expensive educational toys. They received wonderful stimulation from Ping-Pong balls, plastic measuring spoons, plastic containers—any small manipulatable objects. Best books for the crawling set: large ones with stiff cardboard pages. The literature is irrelevant; the point is to engage a baby's fascination with hinged objects.

A Learning Environment: The best parents set up an interesting world for the child and then back off. They identify what the child is interested in rather than trying to focus the child's attention. It does no good to force learning on a child who is not interested at the moment. This only leads to boredom. Better: Wait for the child to come to you. During the crawling stage, that will happen an average of 10 times an hour—whenever the child feels excitement, frustration or pain. Then you'll have a motivated student. In half a minute, you can offer a new idea with a phrase or a toy—and accomplish more than an hour's drill with flash cards.

The best way to teach language skills is the same as it's always been. . . by simply talking, parent to child. Keep your talk concrete and in the present. Relate it to objects the baby can perceive. . . the sock you're putting on, the toy you're holding out. Never use baby talk. But keep in mind the child's limits. Most effective: Talking to children at or slighly beyond their apparent level of understanding.

Reading aloud can also be useful, but only if the child is receptive. Best opportunitiy: Just before bedtime.

Most important advice: Let children develop at their own pace. They need their parents' assistance, but certainly not some rigidly choreographed approach to learning. You may not end up with a five-year-old violin prodigy, but perhaps you'll get something better: A well-rounded, delightful person—short run and long run.

Source: Burton L. White, director, Center for Parent Education, 55 Chapel St., Newton , MA 02160, and author of *The First Three Years of Life*, Prentice-Hall, Englewood Cliffs, NJ 07632.

HOW LIABLE ARE YOU FOR YOUR CHILD'S MISCHIEF?

The issue of who is to blame when your child damages someone else's property or endangers another person is complicated. Children's mischief used to be comparatively mild, and parents tended to pay the damages out of court quietly. But changes in the structure of the family and in society in general have made the question of responsibility more difficult to establish.

Millions of dollars' worth of damage is done to property annually—a high percentage by minors. The growing number of homes where both parents work and depend on day-care centers or makeshift supervision of their children after school contributes to the problem. The legal issue is clouded by joint custody of divorced parents and by children's rights concepts that are concerned with stemming child abuse and neglect.

There is no federal law that directly holds a parent responsible for a child's actions simply because he is the child's parent. However, there is one federal law that can be applied to child/parent situations. If it can be proved that a child was acting as the *agent* of a parent when he committed his crime, the parent is tried as though he had committed the crime himself. (This would apply, for example, to the burglar who used his small child to get through a tiny opening into a house.)

Although statutes differ, case law decisions seem to have established the age of 12 as the point at which a child can be tried in juvenile court. Younger children usually cannot be tried. At 17 or 18, a young person is considered to be an adult and is therefore tried as an adult.

Reasonable control: A parent can be held responsible for a child's mischief if it can be proved that the parent neglected to exercise reasonable control over his child's behavior.

Example: A child has ben caught defacing schoolyard property several times, yet his parents continue to let him play unsupervised after hours on the school playground. In this case, the parents may be taken to court for child neglect. They knew the child was misbehaving but did nothing to control him.

This concept comes from state laws called vicarious liability statutes. Almost every state has some form of vicarious liability law that requires a parent to pay for damages to property up to a certain maximum ($200 to $10,000, depending on the state) if it can be proved that the parent neglected to control the child's behavior. About half the states hold parents liable for personal injuries their child may have inflicted on others.

Several states with large urban populations have implemented such laws to deal specifically with the vandalization of public buildings and transit systems. New Jersey law: If it can be shown that the parents failed to supervise the child, they are liable for up to $1,000 worth of damage done by that child to a public utility plus court costs. The penalty is levied in lieu of charging juvenile deliquency. Many parents pay just to keep their children from having a police record.

Bottom line: If your child gets into trouble by vandalizing property, your best bet is to pay the damages yourself. That keeps the problem out of court and in the family. For more serious crimes, you need a lawyer.

Source: David Schechner, partner, Schechner and Targan, lawyers, 80 Main St., West Orange, NJ 07052.

BEWARE ROCK CONCERT HANGOVERS

Rock fans who attend concerts on school nights will struggle in class the next day. Reason: After bathing their ears and brains with abnormally loud sound, students will be able to hear only lower frequencies in a normal auditory setting. They'll be hearing their teachers as though pillows covered their ears. Their powers of concentration will be adversely affected, and they will not be attuned to the world in general.

Source: Paul Maduale, director, The Listening Center, 1170-R Yonge St., Toronto, Canada M4W 2L9.

DOES EVERYONE NEED A COLLEGE EDUCATION?

A college degree still pays off, even though it is less valued in the job market than it used to be. The cost of a BA yields a 10%–15% return for life. College graduates earn at least 25% more than their peers who have only a high school diploma. And 95% of college graduates are employed one and a half years after graduation.

Source: Alan Wagner, research associate, Center for Educational Research and Policy Studies, State University of New York, Albany 12203.

THE HIGHEST SCORERS ON GRAD SCHOOL TESTS

Liberal arts majors and science majors do better on graduate school tests than professional or occupational majors. Business majors get the worst scores on the business school entry test, and math majors do better than political science majors on the law school admissions test. Theory: Subjects such as math and philosophy teach students to use symbols and to think in structured ways—all helpful in getting good scores on tests.

Source: Study by the National Institute of Education, 639 Brown Bldg., 1200 19 St. NW, Washington, DC 20208.

Your Home

WHAT YOU SHOULD KNOW ABOUT REAL ESTATE AGENTS

Knowing your legal rights and responsibilities when selling your home yourself or through a real estate broker can save you thousands of dollars. . . and a lot of worry and frustration over your own possible wrong moves.

Selling your own home is not an easy task. You need to be able to provide buyers with information about zoning laws, community services, and the condition of your home. Also, you have no security against intrusions by qualified househunters—curiosity seekers, potential thieves and the like.

If you decide to sell with a broker, shop around to find one who is knowledgeable about your community and with whom you feel comfortable.

Sellers' failure to read the legal documents pertaining to brokers' contracts causes most misunderstandings. Special points:

Commissions paid by the seller to the broker are no longer established by any state agency or private trade association (by federal law). The individual brokers set fees for their own offices. Some will negotiate a commission rate, others will not. The law does not require them to.

The listing agreement is a legal document that outlines the understanding between you and the broker about how your home will be listed for sale. It includes your name, the brokers' name, the address of the property, the asking price and other details about the home, as well as the amount of time you are giving the broker to find a buyer (30, 60 or 90 days

is usual). This is a legal document, binding you to its provisions.

Exclusive right to sell is the most common type of listing. The seller pays full commission to the listing broker, regardless of which real estate office brings in the buyer—even if the seller brings in the buyer.

The exclusive agency agreement permits only one broker to offer your property during an agreed-upon time period. However, you may sell the property yourself, with no obligation to the broker, during the same time period. Most agencies will not accept such a listing.

Buyers' cries of misrepresentation or fraud are heard increasingly these days. The seller has a duty to tell the broker about defects in the house that are known to the seller and that might affect a buyer's willingness to purchase the property. Knowing about such defects and not mentioning them invites a suit for misrepresentation or fraud. Honesty may save you future fears and problems.

Lawsuits against sellers and brokers about other problems relating to a house and neighborhood are cropping up. Are you required or is your broker required to disclose that the land beneath the home was once a chemical waste dump, or that you were aware of plans for a sewage-treatment plant down the street? Those kinds of questions are still to be resolved by the courts, but you can see the importance of full disclosure of what you do know.

Signing a contract and accepting a buyer's "earnest" money commit you to the sale—unless the buyer reneges and therefore forfeits the money, or some contingency to the sale negates the contract. If you've signed a contract and then refuse to follow through, you could face a lawsuit should the buyer want to initiate one. In any event, you may still be responsible for the broker's commission.

Source: John R. Linton, vice president, legal affairs, National Association of Realtors, 430 N. Michigan Ave., Chicago 60611.

WHAT YOU SHOULD KNOW ABOUT INSURANCE AND YOUR HOME

• Higher deductibles make sense—and not only for auto coverage. Most people have kept $100 deductibles in their homeowner policies. Go to $250 or $500, and use the savings to pay for a bigger policy. Or go from contents coverage to a superior replacement-cost basis. Rule of thumb: You can generally afford to risk a deductible equal to one week's after-tax salary.

Source: *Working Woman,* 600 Madison Ave., New York 10022.

• A college student's valuables may be best insured by personal-article "floaters". These extend standard homeowner policies. Most reasonable rates: Stereos, cameras and musical instruments. Bonus: Floaters provide coverage for loss or accidental damage as well as for theft.

Source: *Sylvia Porter's Personal Finance,* 380 Lexington Ave., New York 10017.

• Telephone-wiring insurance—sold for a monthly fee by local phone companies—is not a wise buy. Inside phone wiring rarely needs repairs. Handy owners or electricians can fix it themselves. Apartment dwellers often will be protecting only a few inches of wire. Behind the new insurance: Since the AT&T divestiture, homeowners are responsible for their inside wiring. Bell decided to charge for repairs.

KEEPING YOUR HOME SAFE

• A multipurpose dry chemical unit is the best home fire extinguisher. Check the label to see what kinds of fires it's effective against. It should cover Class A (ordinary combustibles like wood and cloth), Class B (gases, greases, flammable liquids) and Class C (electrical fires).

• Smoke detectors work best in a two-unit system. Place an ionization detector in the hallway outside your bedroom for a quick alert on a racing fire. Then install a photoelectric model downstairs in the general living area or in the main stairway that will detect smoke from smoldering upholstery or rugs.

• Aluminum wiring, which was used in two million homes and apartments built between 1965 and 1973. The wiring has caused more than 500 home fires in the last 10 years. To check: Ask the original electrical contractor, or look for an "AL" stamp on exposed wires in your basement. If you do have aluminum wiring, a qualified electrician may be able to make your house safe at a moderate cost. Never attempt repairs (even simple ones) on your own.

Source: *Consumer Adviser,* Reader's Digest Association, Inc., Pleasantville, NY 10570.

RECOMMENDATIONS OF A MASTER LOCKSMITH

Today's burglars are more sophisticated than ever. Unfortunately, since the authorities are locking up so few burglars, we have to lock ourselves up.

There is such a bewildering variety of locks and other security devices on the market today that it's hard to know what to buy. Some cheaper models are as good as more expensive ones. Here are some tips on home security, including which products do the best job for the least money.

Lock and door security: Traditional wisdom says there's no point in putting a good lock on a flimsy door. This is not true. In most cases you must prove forcible entry to collect insurance. If you have a poor lock, your cylinder can be picked in seconds. You're inviting your insurance company to give you a hard time. The best strategies:

• Put a piece of sheet steel on your door if it has panels on it. If the panels are glass, replace them with Lexon, an unbreakable plastic.

• If you have a wooden door, get what the industry calls a police lock. This is a brace lock with a bar that goes from the lock into the floor about 30 inches away from the base of the door. Our favorite: Magic Eye. Its new model can be locked from the inside like the old model, but you can get out easily in an emergency. Also: Get a police lock if your door frame is weak. It keeps the door from giving because of the brace in the floor. Even the best regular locks won't protect you if the whole frame gives.

• If you're buying a door, buy a metal flush door without panels, and get an equally strong frame to match it. What makes a good frame: A hollow metal construction, same as the door.

• If your door opens out instead of in, get a double bar lock—one that extends horizontally on each side. With a door that opens out, the hinges are often exposed on the outside, allowing a burglar to remove the door from its hinges. With a double bar lock he can't pull the door out.

Other important devices include:

• Plates: Pulling out the lock cylinder is the burglar's easiest and most effective way of getting in. Most people put a plate over their lock and think that will take care of it. But most plates have bolts that are exposed on the outside. With a hollow metal door, the burglar can pull that plate away from the door with a wedge and simply cut the bolts. If the head of the bolt is exposed, he can pull it out slightly with pliers and snap it right off. Remedy: Medeco's Bodyguard. A cylinder and plate combination, it's a drill-resistant, one-piece unit with no exposed bolts, a sleeve to prevent burglars from chiseling the bolts, and a hardened plate to protect the keyhole. A Segal lock is the best choice for this system.

• Jimmy bars: Don't bother with them. They're psychological protection only. If you have a metal door, a good lock is sufficient protection. With a metal door, we recommend a jimmy bar only if the door has been damaged through a forcible break-in and is separated from the frame. In this case the bar will straighten out the door and hide some of the light shining through. If you have a wooden door, a jimmy bar can actually help a burglar by giving him leverage. He can put a crowbar up against it, dig into the wood and break through the door.

• Peepholes: Get one that's as small as possible. Large peepholes use a one-way mirror that doesn't permit you to see around corners. And if someone hits that mirror while you're looking through, it could damage your eye. Small peepholes use a double lens, making it possible to see around corners. And if the small peephole is knocked off the door, it won't benefit the burglar. If a big one is knocked off, it creates a weakness in your security. Recommended: If you already have a large peephole, remove it. Have the locksmith bolt two plates on the door, with a smaller hole in the center to accommodate a small peephole.

• Closets: Let's say you want to protect a closet—not necessarily against burglars, but against someone who might have a key to your house or apartment. Locking the closet isn't sufficient, because most closets open out and have hinges on the outside, making it easy to remove the door. Remedy: A door pin. This involves putting the pin on the hinge side of the door and through a receiving hole in the frame. Anyone who cut the hinges off or removed their pins couldn't lift the door out.

• Window locks: The best window locks use a key, which makes them difficult to manipulate from the outside. Without a key, any window lock is vulnerable. Best: One with a heavy pin that allows you to drill holes for either complete locking or three- or six-inch ventilation. Our favorite: Lok Safe.

• Window gate: In New York and other cities the fire laws prohibit window gates that lock with a key. Remedy: Gates with keyless locks. They allow you to get out easily, but a burglar can't put his hand through the gate to open it. Our favorite: P·A·G window gates.

When you're choosing a locksmith, go to locksmith's shops to size them up. Make sure the store is devoted exclusively to the locksmith business and isn't just doing locksmithing on the side. Ask to see the locksmith's license if it's not displayed. There are a lot of unlicensed people doing business illegally. Best: Locksmiths who belong to an association. They are keeping up with the latest developments. Look for a sticker in the window indicating membership in a local or national locksmith's association.

Source: Sal Schillizzi of All-Over Locksmiths, Inc., 1189 Lexington Ave., New York 10028.

HOUSEHOLD HINTS MOTHER DIDN'T TELL YOU

• Nicked crystal glassware can be restored. Rub the rough edge with an emery board or fine nailfile.

• Clearing your walk goes much faster if you coat your snow shovel with automotive wax or a nonstick cooking spray. This makes the snow fall off easily.

Source: *Family Handyman*, 205 E. 42 St., New York 10017.

• Ballpoint-ink stains can be removed from washable fabrics by spraying with hair spray and then blotting up the spot.

Source: *Playboy*, 919 N. Michigan Ave., Chicago 60611.

• A dropped contact lens doesn't require blindly groping around the floor. Better strategy: First, make sure the lens isn't hiding under an eyelid. Then turn out the lights and shine a flashlight where you dropped the lens. The tiny glass should reflect the light, revealing its location. For hard lenses only: Pull a pantyhose leg over the nozzle of a vacuum cleaner and sweep the area where the lens fell. It will be sucked up against the pantyhose.

• A fluorescent light must stay off at least 15 minutes to save on electricity costs. But it always pays to turn off incandescent lights.

Source: *Working Woman*, 342 Madison Ave., New York 10173.

• If you need a strong light, use one brighter bulb rather than several weaker ones. Fact: One 100-watt incandescent bulb produces more light than two 60-watt bulbs, yet consumes 20% less energy.

Source: Nancy Christensen, residential lighting specialist, General Electric Co., Nela Park, Cleveland 44112.

• Tea kettle deposits can be dissolved with a solution of white vinegar and water—half and half. Boil for five minutes and let stand overnight. Rinse the kettle thoroughly

Source: *Food & Wine*, 90 Park Ave., New York 10016.

• When washing windows, use vertical strokes on one side of the pane and horizontal strokes on the other. That way you will be able to locate any remaining streaks.

• Avoid refrigerator repairs by regularly vacuuming the condenser coils. Dusty buildups can cause the unit to overheat and even shut down. Especially vulnerable: Refrigerators on bare floors.

Source: *Good Housekeeping*.

• To see if an oriental-rug is authentic, spread the pile apart. If you see knots at the bottom, the rug was made by hand. But sewn-on fringess are a clear machine-made giveaway.

Source: Pasargad, Inc., rug importers and manufacturers, 1351 Connecticut Ave., NW, Washington, DC 20036.

COMMON IN-HOME DANGERS

• Indoor pollution may be as much as 10 times worse than outdoor pollution. Most common pollutants: Asbestos. . .carbon monoxide. . .sulfur dioxide. . .formaldehyde (especially in new homes built of plywood and other cheap materials). . .aerosol sprays. . .cleaning products. . .dry-cleaning chemicals. . .and cosmetics. Highest risk: Well-insulated homes that trap pollutants inside.

Source: Report by the Consumer Product Safety Commission, in *Moneysworth*.

• Wood-burning stoves can cause respiratory problems in pre-schoolage children, according to results of a Michigan study. Reason: Unclear.

Source: *Medical World News*, 211 E. 43 St., New York 10017.

• Bathtub electrocutions are often caused by appliances that aren't turned on at the time. If an appliance is plugged in and falls into the tub, the water will complete the circuit. Most frequent cause of electrocution deaths: Hair driers.

Source: *Good Housekeeping*

Your Car

USED-CAR TRAPS

• Used-car buyers, beware: Odometer tampering is a lot more prevalent than most people think. About three million of the 18 million used cars sold each year have had their odometers rolled back. Average rollback, 30,000 miles—which boosts prices for most cars about $75/car.

Source: National Highway Traffic Safety Administration.

• Buy a used car during the day. (Night lighting can make cars look more attractive than they are.) Don't shop in the rain. (Rain can mask leaking liquids). Best season: Winter, when supplies are high and demand is low.

AVOID THE RUSTPROOFING TRAP

Dealer-applied rustproofing should be done as soon as you buy the car. But be careful. Read the fine print. Most "guarantees" give you only the cost of rustproofing in case of rust. Make sure the guarantee states that the dealer will repair or replace rusted body panels.

Some rustproofers demand that you return every year at a strictly specified time in order to keep the guarantee in effect. They'll usually hit you with a $25 refresher-application bill. Find a rustroofer who will give you at least a month's leeway on that return date.

Rip-off artists simply drill the holes and put in a plastic plug, never applying the rustproofing agent at all. When you get the car home, take off the plugs and insert a screwdriver in the holes. The agent, still a little runny, will come off on the screwdriver. If it's not there, get your money back.

You can save money with a do-it-yourself rustproofing kit. You'll probably do a more conscientious job than a mechanic anyway, and the materials are equal in quality.

AUTO LEMONAID

If that new car you just bought has been in the shop more than on the road, don't despair. Under state "lemon laws" (in force in 19 states and pending in 20 others), you may be able to get most of your money back, or at least a more reliable car. . .and without the risk of heavy court costs.

The law: The car is usually covered for one year or the written warranty period, whichever is shorter. If a defect isn't repaired in four tries, the manufacturer must replace the car or give a refund (less depreciation). The same goes if the car is out of commission for 30 days or more for any combination of defects. If the manufacturer has a federally approved arbitration program, you must first submit your complaint to the arbitrators. But if you aren't satisfied with their decision, you can still take the company to court.

If you think you have a case:

• Check the state attorney general's office for details of the law. Key point: Whether the manufacturer (as well as the dealer) must be given a chance to solve the problem.
• Submit a list of repairs to the dealer each time you bring the car in. Keep a copy for yourself.
• Keep a detailed record of car-repair dates and of periods when the car was unavailable to you.
• If the company agrees to settle but offers too little money or a car with too many miles, don't be afraid to dicker. The company doesn't

want to go to court any more than you do.

Source: *Medical Economics*, Box 552, Oradell, NJ 07649.

WINTER DRIVING

To get unstuck: Try turning your wheels from side to side to push away the snow. Check to be sure that your tailpipe is clear (so carbon monoxide won't be forced into the car). Start the motor, put the car in gear, and apply slow, steady pressure to the accelerator to allow the tires to get a grip. Don't spin the wheels (this just digs you in further). Let the car pull out straight ahead if possible. Extra help: Sprinkle kitty litter in front of the wheels for traction.

To brake on ice: Start early. Squeeze the brakes with a steady pressure until just before you feel them begin to lock. Ease up, and slowly repeat the pressure. Disc brakes do not respond well to pumping (the old recommendation for drum brakes). They will lock, causing you to lose control of the car.

To recover from a skid: Take your feet off both the accelerator pedal and the brake pedal. Hold the wheel firmly, but keep the steering adjustments to a minimum. Oversteering can cause you to fishtail. Slamming on the brakes takes away all steering control.

Source: National Safety Council, 444 N. Michigan Ave., Chicago 60611.

THE SAFEWAY TO TRAVEL

• The safest car travel: In a heavy car whose occupants are wearing seat belts. A new study found that belts reduce the risk of injury by two-thirds. Also: The injury risk drops another 25% with every additional thousand pounds of car weight.

Source: Insurance Institute for Highway Safety, 600 New Hampshire Ave. NW, Washington DC 20037.

• Seat-belt myth: Passengers are better off being thrown clear of their car in a serious accident. Reality: You are 25 times more likely to be killed if thrown from the car.

Source: National Traffic Safety Institute.

• Seat belts are vital to auto safety even when you're traveling slowly. Four out of five fatal or serious car accidents involve cars going less than 40 miles per hour.

Source: Jane Brody in *The New York Times*.

WHERE THE GAS GOES

Your car's gas mileage can be dramatically affected by options, by road conditions and even by weather. These are the chief enemies of fuel economy:

• Cold weather (1%–2% drop for each 10°F.).
• Rain or powerful headwinds (10% or more).
• Winding roads, steep grades (about 33% for a 3% grade).
• Rough surfaces (15%–35%).
• Heavy loads (1%–3% for each 100 pounds).
• Poor engine tuning (5%–20%).
• High speeds (15%–20% at 70 miles per hour versus 50 miles per hour).
• Automatic transmission (2%–6%).

Source: *Reader's Digest Consumer Adviser*, Reader's Digesst Association, Inc., Pleasantville, NY 10570.

WORST TIMES TO DRIVE

The worst time to drive is between midnight and 3 am. You're 13 times more likely to have a fatal car accident than between 6 am and 6 pm. Most dangerous hour: From 2 am to 3 am on Sunday morning (after the bars close)—your chance of a fatal accident then is 22 times higher.

Source: Study by Sherman Stein, professor of mathematics, University of California at Davis.

HANGOVER HAZARD

Even after eight hours of sleep following a night of heavy drinking, you should not drive a car. Driving ability is impaired as much as 20% the morning after a bender—whether you feel rotten or not. Your reactions are slowed down after a bout of drinking alcohol even if your head and stomach have escaped the classic hangover symptoms. Stay away from the wheel until afternoon at least.

Source: Study by the Swedish National Road and Traffic Institute reported in *Journal of the American Medical Association*.

Travel and Vacation

SURPRISE TRAVEL AGENT FEES

Travel agents are beginning to charge for services they once provided free: Itinerary planning, passport preparation and economy-travel arrangements. Some have moved to consultation fees as high as $50 an hour. Bottom line: Check on the price before you ask an agent to research low fares on tours for you.

INSIDER'S GUIDE TO AIR TRAVEL

• Airline meal options now range from the diet-oriented (low calorie, low cholesterol, diabetic, salt-free) to the ethnic (kosher, Mormon, Hindu, Moslem) to vegetarian and seafood choices. To get what you want, call the airline at least 48 hours before take-off time.
Source: *U.S. News & World Report.*

• Even with airline deregulation, you're still protected when you're involuntarily bumped from an overbooked flight. What they owe you: For delays over one hour, compensation equal to ticket price, up to $200. For delays over two hours, it goes to twice the ticket price, up to $400. New policy: You're not entitled to compensation if the airline can get you to your destination within an hour of original arrival time. And while some airlines still provide meals and lodging over long delays, they're no longer obliged to.
Source: *Better Homes and Gardens.*

• Clearing airport security. (1) Don't pack anything that even remotely resembles a weapon—including scissors or a picnic knife. (2) Leave some room inside carry-on baggage. If the inspectors open it, it will be easier to repack. (3) Pack gifts without gift-wrap so they can be seen. (4) Carry film and loaded cameras in a separate bag for hand inspection unless you keep them in protective lead bags.

• Airline tickets are not covered by insurance. If yours is lost or stolen, you'll have to buy a new one. Then, if the original ticket hasn't been used, you'll be reimbursed for the second ticket less a $20–$30 charge. There is, of course, a claim form to fill out, and a wait of six to eight weeks.

• Lost airline tickets. You can be reimbursed if the ticket isn't used or cashed in before its expiration date (usually 90 days to one year after the date of issue). Report the loss at once to the airline or travel agent that issued the ticket. For a faster refund: Report the ticket number.
Source: *McCall's.*

• Delays at airports are making membership in airline clubs even more desirable. Cost: $40–$130/year. Typical services: Free check cashing, message service, free local phone calls, favored reservation numbers, and access to meting rooms and private club lounges.

ECONOMY TRAVEL TIMES

• Economy vacation. Off-season Caribbean hotel rates are 30%–50% off peak levels through mid-December. Air fares are discounted too.
Source: Tourism Association, 20 E. 46 St., New York 10017.

• Check weekend hotel rates in non-resort areas. They're often much lower than weekday rates.
• Bargain accommodations in college dormitory rooms are available to summer travelers. Facilities usually include food service and parking, and are near campus cultur-

al and recreational activities. Also available: Dorm rooms at 230 universities in 25 foreign countries. In England alone, 50 schools offer bed and breakfast.

Source: *U.S. and Worldwide Travel Accommodations Guide*, Campus Travel Service, 1303 E. Balboa Blvd., Newport Beach, CA 92661.

• Off-season bargain: Europe offers a lot. The winters are relatively mild...orchestras and opera companies are in season...museum lines are short...top restaurants receive you without reservations. Best of all, hotel and transportation prices often are far below their midseason peaks. Example: The Grand Hotel in Rome, which runs $220 a day in summer, costs only $110 a day in winter.

Source: *Sylvia Porter's Personal Finance*, 380 Lexington Ave., New York 10017.

SMART ALTERNATIVES TO TRAVELER'S CHECKS

Credit cards are now better than traveler's checks for most trips overseas. Aside from the cards' convenience, they save as much as 6% on exchange costs. Best bet: Visa, with a conversion markup only one-quarter of 1% above the wholesale bank currency rate. Other major cards carry a 1% markup—still far better than the 3% or more you'd pay for retail markups on traveler's checks.

Exceptions: Poorer European countries such as Spain and Third World countries, where dollar-hungry bankers often give a break on traveler's checks or cash.

Source: *Forbes.*

WHERE THE INTERNATIONAL BANKERS STAY

In Europe: The Vier Jahreszeiten (Hamburg), Dolder Grand (Zurich), Connaught (London), Ritz (Madrid), and Hassler Villa Medici (Rome).

In Asia: The Oriental (Bangkok), Mandarin (Hong Kong), Okura (Tokyo), Shangri-La (Singapore), and Regent (Hong Kong).

In North America: Ritz Carlton (Chicago), Four Seasons (Washington, DC), Carlyle (New York), Four Seasons (Toronto), and Stanford Court (San Francisco).

Source: *Institutional Investor*, 488 Madison Ave., New York 10022.

DANGEROUS GESTURING

Gesturing when abroad may get you into unexpected trouble. Often the American meaning of a gesture is much more innocent than its European counterpart. Example: The OK sign (thumb and forefinger in a circle) means "you're worth zero" in France and Belgium and is a vulgar insult in Italy, and Greece and Turkey. Bottom line: Use gestures cautiously while you're abroad.

Source: Study by paul ekman, professor of psychology, University of California at San Francisco, quoted in *U.S. News and World Report.*

TIPPING IN EUROPE

In most European restaurants *Service included* is printed on the menu, so just add a few small coins if you wish. Otherwise—in Portugal, for example—tip 15%–20% of the bill, excluding tax, as in the U.S. The wine steward gets 10% of the wine bill in most places, although his fee is included in the bill in Germany and Switzerland. In a hotel, give the chambermaid $1 if her service isn't included in the bill. Bellmen get the equivalent of 25¢–50¢ per bag, and helpful doormen about 50¢. For taxis, tip 10%–15 of the meter in most countries; service is included in Belgium, Switzerland, Scandinavia and the Netherlands.

Source: *Travel & Leisure.*

MEDICAL INSURANCE OVERSEAS

Most US plans cover you when you travel abroad for the same services provided here. (You may have to pay and get reimbursed later.) Check your policy, noting especially any territorial exclusions. Major exception: Medicare offers no overseas protection, except under special circumstances in Mexico and Canada.

If you're not covered abroad: Buy short-term evacuation and/or hospital insurance for the length of your trip. Evacuation insurance pays to get you to a hospital back home in case of an emergency. Hospital insurance covers care for injuries and illness sustained abroad. NEAR,* a membership organization, specializes in evacuation insurance. Health Care Abroad** combines evacuation and hospital insurance. Other packages sold through travel agents inlcude indemnity coverage with health coverage. No US insurance policy covers treatments abroad that aren't covered here.

1900 N. MacArthur Blvd., Oklahoma City, OK 73127.

**1029 Investment Bldg., 1511 K St. NW, Washington, DC 20005.

WHEN IT'S DANGEROUS TO FLY

• Don't-fly basics: Those who have had a heart attack within four weeks of take-off. . .a stroke within two weeks. . .surgery within two weeks. . .or a deep-diving session within 24 hours should wait to fly. Don't fly at all if you have severe lung problems. . .uncontrolled hypertension. . . epilepsy not well controlled. . .severe anemia. . .a pregnancy beyond 240 days or threatened by miscarriage.

Source: *Pocket Flight Guide/Frequent Flyer Package,* 2000 Clearwater Dr., Oak Brook, IL 60521.

• Flying can be hazardous for victims of chronic obstructive pulmonary disease. Reason: Sudden changes in atmospheric pressure can deplete oxygen levels in the bloodstream. Possible consequences: Shortness of breath, dizziness, collapse and even heart arrhythmias. Pulmonary disease sufferers should have blood-oxygen levels checked several days before a scheduled flight.

Source: *Medical World News,* 211 E. 43 St., New York 10017.

TRUTH ABOUT STATE LOTTERIES

State lotteries are one of the worst bets around. They claim that about 50% of the money wagered is returned as prizes. In fact,

considering the lotteries' deferred-payment schedules (a $1 million prize is awarded as $50,000 a year for 20 years), the payout actually comes to less than 25%. Comparison: In Nevada or Atlantic City, the payout in roulette is about 94%.

Source: *The Wall Street Journal.*

HOW NOT TO MAKE GAMBLING MISTAKES

To have any real chance of success in Nevada or Atlantic City, you must learn money management. Good plan for casual players: Find out what your minimum bet can be and bring at least 100–125 times that amount to last your total stay. With any less you won't be able to play comfortably.

My basic plan applies to blackjack, craps, roulette or whatever game you play. Let's say you start with $400, which has to last a weekend. Divide that stake into four parts. This leaves you $100 per gambling session—the bare minimum for survival at a five-dollar table. (Important: You *never* draw from one session's stake to replenish another.)

There are three possibilities:

• You lose the $100 quickly. Leave the table, and the casino, to clear your head for the next session.
• After 30 minutes of slow-but-steady losing, you find you're down to $50. Cash in your chips and take at least a 30-minute break. Never play more than a half-hour at a losing session.
• You're in luck and you're winning good. Goal: To preserve your profits, rather than sitting at the table until you give it all back. Good rule: As soon as you've doubled your money (to $200), put your original $100 in your pocket, not to be touched until you see the cashier. Now you're in the ideal situation: Playing with the casino's money. If your luck sours, quit when you've lost 25% of your profits—in this case $25. If you manage to run your profits to $200, quit after losing $50, and so on. Although it's hard to leave when you're still ahead, this kind of discipline separates potential winners from inevitable losers.

Of course, many players beat themselves before they ever make that profit. Their most common mistakes:

• Making "flat bets"—wagering the same amount each time. Since the odds are against you, your progress will soon resemble a sales chart in a recession . . . peaks and valleys, but down in the long run. Try a simple progression: Bet one unit (the table minimum) to start. If you win, you go to two units . . . if you win again, to three . . . then back to one. (There are other, more aggressive progressions.) If you lose at any point, you start over again. Goal: To maximize your profits in a winning streak but cut your losses when you're cold.

• Trying to get even by chasing their losses with meal money . . . or the next month's rent.

• Flitting from craps to baccarat to the slots. It's better to stick with one game until you're comfortable.

• Taking too many long-shot bets (such as "proposition" bets in craps). They generally offer the worst odds.

• Staying at a "cold" table too long. Atlantic City is probably the cleanest gambling town in the world. (It's almost impossible for blackjack dealers there to cheat, since they deal from their shoes.) But if a new dealer is giving you terrible cards, or there's a loudmouth across the table, or you don't like the smell of your neighbor's cigar, feel free to move on.

• Accepting complimentary alcohol.

• Playing when they're tired.

• Getting caught up in the casino mentality. When everyone refers to $5 as a "nickel" and $25 as a "quarter," it's easy to treat money like plastic.

• Viewing the dealer as a shark who's out to get them. That's just foolsh. At worst, the dealer is a mechanical device. At best, he can be your ally.

Source: Lee Pantano, a professional gambler, teacher and consultant. His column, *Casino Line,* is published in New Jersey, and his cable television show of the same name is seen in six states and Canada.

HOW TO GET VIP TREATMENT AT THE WHITE HOUSE

Most people think that the only way they will ever enter the White House is by joining the tourists and waiting on line for hours. That's true, *unless* you know the system.

• Best bet . . .

How to be part of a special VIP tour: Contact your Representative or Senator. But plan ahead. There are only a few of these tickets available at any given time. Give your Congressman plenty of advance warning.

• Long shot . . .

How to get invited to a special function: Find out who is being entertained or honored at state dinners or celebrations. For information, call the Office of The Press Secretary (202-456-2100). If an appropriate event is scheduled, call the Office of Public Liaison (202-456-6286) and explain who you are and why you should be invited.

Example: Suppose your business exports agricultural machinery. You find out that a Middle Eastern Sheik and his delegation, including his Minister of Agriculture is being hosted by the President at a formal dinner. You call the Office of Public Liaison and ask to be invited. Point out that you are an expert in agribusiness, know about the problems of doing business overseas, and can be an asset both in terms of interacting with the guests, and in terms of forwarding American interests overseas.

Of course, if you are known as a worker for, or a member of an organization or cause sponsored by the First Lady, there are other sources of invitations.

Example: If the First Lady is an advocate for abused women, and you are involved in establishing shelters for them, try calling the Office of the The First Lady (202-456-7136). Find out when she will be hosting the next gathering of advocates and make a case for being invited.

Finally, devoted party workers and important contributors, are often rewarded by an invitation—if they ask to be.

Sex

SECRETS OF MAN-WOMAN FRIENDSHIPS

• Most men—whether married or single—believe a real friendship with a woman is impossible without sex. But women generally seek close platonic relationships with both sexes.

Source: Study by Dr. Gerald Phillips, professor of speech communication, Penn State University.

• Man-woman friendships are far more common now than they were 20 years ago. Reasons: Since people are marrying later, they turn to friends of the opposite sex for the companionship they are missing. And with more occupations open to both sexes, men and women have more shared interests.

Source: Dr. Marilyn Ruman, a psychologist in Encino, CA.

MALE/FEMALE MYTHS

• Ignorance about sex doesn't make people less promiscuous. Rather, it makes them feel guiltier—and more likely to have impulsive, unprotected sex. Lack of knowledge leads to irresponsible sexual behavior. Research finding: Sex education classes do little to change students' overall values.

Source: Robert Pollack, professor of psychology, University of Georgia, in *Self*.

• Sex myth: Thanks to the women's movement and the sexual "revolution," extramarital sex has become commonplace. Fact: The American marriage remains highly traditional. In one study, more than 70% of marriage partners had never had an extra-marital affair.

Source: Frederick Humphrey, marriage researcher at the University of Connecticut and past president of the American Association of Marriage and Family Therapy.

• When asked how many sexual partners the average mid-thirties female would have had, women estimated 18–30. But men said the typical woman would have had only three to nine partners. Theory: Men are uncomfortable with the notion of "double digit" women—even when they've had that much experience themselves.

Source: Carol Cassell, president of the American Association for Sex Educators, Counselors and Therapists.

• Male-virility myths notwithstanding, women are more likely to complain that a penis is too large than too small. Reason: Intercourse can become uncomfortable for a woman when penetration is too deep.

Source: Dr. Theresa L. Crenshaw, director, The Crenshaw Clinic, San Diego, in *Medical Aspects of Human Sexuality*, 360 Lexington Ave., New York 10017.

ALL ABOUT KISSING

• Whether it's a peck on Aunt Sadie's cheek or a deep, romantic clinch with your spouse, kissing is a universal communication that says many things. Added benefit: In a study by a West German life insurance company, men who kissed their wives every morning before going to work were found to live longer, healthier lives than the average. Examples of style:
• The French kiss. This originated with an ancient Chinese belief that a woman has a "jade spring" of vitality under her tongue that a man can tap by kissing her. It is still the most popular form of kissing between lovers.
• Warm, open kiss. Leaves room to get passionate or to stay friendly (your partner can decide).
• Kiss on the cheek. A cordial and warm greeting.

• Soft, brief kiss. Shows affection but not necessarily passion.

Source: Danny Biederman, author of *The Book of Kisses*, Dembner Enterprises Corp., 1841 Broadway, New York 10023.

TECHNIQUES FOR BETTER SEX

Five "T"s for good sex: Trust, touch, time, tease and talk. Key ingredient: The "talk" must be in bed and about sex. Ritual silence during love-making can only impede change, variety and maximum enjoyment.

Source: Dr. Domeena Renshaw, Director, Loyola University Sex Clinic, Maywood, IL, in *Medical Aspects of Human Sexuality*.

• The pleasures of petting were missed by many modern couples when the sexual revolution relaxed the restriciton on premarital intercourse. Happy revival: Leaders of sex seminars report a renewed interest in the techniques of foreplay—the kind of necking activity previous generations spent years perfecting before marriage. The joys of hand holding, hugging, stroking and French kissing are making a comeback.

Source: Sharon Goldsmith, RN, a Los Angeles sex educator and host of *Human Sexuality* on the Cable Health Network.

• Sexual boredom often afflicts men with the most active sex and fantasy lives. Sex becomes a merry-go-round leading nowhere, eventually leaving them dissatisfied or impotent. Causes: Promiscuous, superficial sex. . .a preoccupation with pornography. . .performance anxiety. . .a fear of commitment. Treatment: Open communication (outside of sex) with a partner the man truly cares about.

Source: Lorna and Philip Sarrel, codirectors of the Yale Human Sexuality Program, in *Gentleman's Quarterly*.

• Overlong intercourse can be more painful than exciting for women. Comfortable limit for many women: 10–15 minutes of continuous thrusting. More than that, even with adequate lubrication, might cause soreness and discomfort.

Source: *Bedside Manners* by Dr. Teresa Larson Crenshaw, Pinnacle Books, 1430 Broadway, New York 10018.

SEXUAL FANTASIES

• Sexual fantasies don't have to be of the whips-and-chains variety. By liberating the imagination, even simple fantasies such as pretending to be in an exotic place or role-playing a character you would like to be can add playfulness to a relationship. Fantasies can allow partners to communicate real needs in a non-threatening way. A good start for the shy: Write down a fantasy in detail and read it aloud to your partner.

Source: *How to Make Love to Each Other* by Alexandra Penny, G.P. Putnam & Sons, 200 Madison Ave., New York 10016.

• Most common sexual fantasies (for heterosexual men): Replacement of the established partner. Forced sexual encounters with women. Observing others' sexual activity. Sexual encounters with men. Group sex. Among homosexual men, sexual encounters with women represent the third most common fantasy.

Source: Study by Drs. Mark Schwartz and William Masters in *American Journal of Psychiatry*, 1700 18 St., NW, Washington, DC 20009.

• Men's sexual fantasies are being affected by the women's liberation movement. College-aged men today are more titillated by sexual stories in which the male and female partners are equally asssertive than they are by descriptions of dominant-passive situations.

Source: Study by Mark Sirkin of the University of Connecticut at Storrs, presented at the annual meeting of the Society for the Scientific Study of Sex.

ORGASM

• Orgasms are faked by men as well as by women. Reasons: Fatigue and the desire to sleep; concern that they can't achieve a second orgasm in the same session; protection of their partner's feelings or their own egos.

Source: Research by sex therapists Linda Levine and Lonnie Barbach, cited in *Mademoiselle*.

• Women and sex. Only about 30% of women reach orgasm during intercourse. Another 30% have orgasms only with masturbation (by themselves or with their lovers).

Another 30% have virtually no orgasms at all. And 5% have emotional problems that make orgasm impossible. Key: A woman must feel free to teach a man what gives her pleasure.

Source: Dr. Ruth Westheimer, sex therapist and adjunct associate professor at New York Hospital—Cornell University in *Playboy*.

SEX AND AGING

Contrary to general belief, sex remains a vital part of most people's lives into their seventies and even beyond. A survey of 4,246 men and women aged 50—93 found that:

• More than 75% of married couples in their sixties have intercourse. Average frequency: Once a week.
• More than three-quarters of single men (widowed, divorced or never married) remain sexually active in their seventies. So do half the single women that age.
• Six out of 10 married couples in their seventies still have regular intercourse. Average frequency: Three times a month.
• Common ailments (arthritis, diabetes, heart disease) cause little decline in sexual activity.

Source: *Love, Sex and Aging: A Consumers Union Report* by Edward M. Brecher and the editors of Consumer Reports Books, Little, Brown and Co., 34 Beacon St., Boston 02106.

SEX AND MEN OVER 50

Sexual dysfunction. The most common causes, according to a study of men over 50, are the use of antihypertension medication (reported by 18% of those surveyed)... prostate surgery (13%)... heart attack (10%) ...diabetes (6%). Leading causes in women: Hysterectomy (34%)...ovariectomy (removal of both ovaries) (18%)...antihypertension medication (18%)...mastectomy (5%)...diabetes (4%)...heart attack (4%).

Source: *Love, Sex and Aging: A Consumers Union Report* by Edward M. Brecher and the editors of Consumer Reports Books, Little, Brown and Co., 34 Beacon St., Boston 02106.

SEXUAL PROBLEMS

An aphrodisiac drug may soon be widely available. The knowledge exists for its development. It is only a matter of time until its production. The drug stimulates the chemicals in the brain responsible for libido and pleasure. Object: To treat people who have trouble becoming sexually excited.

Source: Helen Singer Kaplan, MD, Director, Human Sexuality Teaching Program, The New York Hospital-Cornell Medical Center, New York, addressing the World Congress of Sexology in Washington.

• Older men who have trouble attaining erections at night can do better with morning sex. Testosterone levels are higher earlier in the day.

Source: *Medical Aspects of Human Sexuality*, 360 Lexington Ave., New York 10017.

• At least 20% of sexual problems have physical causes. In a recent British study, many women with orgasm problems were found to have a minor nerve defect that weakened a clitoral reflex.

Source: Dr. Alan Wabrek, Hartford Hospital, Hartford, CT 06115.

• Vaginal lubrication in sexually stimulated women decreases sharply after menopause, with 40% of post-menopausal women describing their lubrication as "inadequate" for sexual intercourse. Two simple solutions: More foreplay...use of a commercially prepared sexual lubricant.

Source: *Love, Sex and Aging* by Edward M. Brecher and the editors of Consumer Reports Books, 256 Washington St., Mt. Vernon, NY 10550.

• Vaginismus is an involutary spasm of muscles near the vaginal opening. Commonly misdiagnosed, it makes intercourse painful or even impossible. Treatment: A combination of limited psychotherapy and supervised dilation usually works within two to three months.

Source: *Bedside Manners* by Dr. Theresa Larsen Crenshaw, Pinnacle Books, 1430 Broadway, New York 10018.

• Post-orgasm headaches often reflect a troubled relationship. Reason: Repressed emotional stress and anxiety often surface as physical ailments. Tension headaches may result if a person senses a lack of warmth or sharing with a spouse—a condition most acute and obvious just after love-making. Common victims: People who are competitive, perfectionist or inarticulate about feelings. Women are affected more often because they are less likely to vent their anger verbally or to make sexual requests. Treatment: Psychotherapy and/or marital counseling, heat and massage, muscle-relaxing tranquilizers. Other headache causes: A sedentary lifestyle, hypertension, performance anxiety or migrane.

Source: *Harper's Bazaar.*

SOME TRUTHS ABOUT IMPOTENCE

• Male impotence can be caused by a zinc deficiency, according to a recent study of dialysis patients. After 50 milligrams of zinc acetate daily for six months, the men's sperm counts and serum testosterone were up significantly. The men also had improved sex drive and more frequent intercourse.

Source: *Vegetarian Times*, 41 E. 42 St., New York 10017.

• Prescription drugs were the villains for 25% of men with impotence problems, a recent study concluded. Possible sex spoilers: Topical antibiotics, anti-histamines, blood pressure medications, anti-anxiety drugs (such as Valium) and anti-depressants. If drugs and lessened desire coincide: Ask your doctor about alternative medications.

Source: *Self.*

• When impotence has a physical basis, the leading cause is arteriosclerosis in the small blood vessels of the penis. Bottom line: The same measures that prevent heart attack—keeping blood pressure and cholesterol levels down—will help ward off impotence as well.

Source: Dr. Helen Singer Kaplan, clinical professor of psychiatry, The New York Hospital-Cornell Medical Center, New York 10021.

• Vasectomy does not lead to later impotence, according to a six-year study of 10,590 vasectomized men. The results, which con-

tradicted an earlier, smaller study at UCLA, found that 162 of the men developed impotence or sexual dysfunction five to 14 years after the operation. That compared well with 155 men in an equal-sized control group.

Source: Report by Dr. Frank J. Massey, professor of biostatistics at the UCLA School of Public Health, in *Medical World News*, 211 E. 43 St., New York 10017.

• Cigarette smoking can be a prime factor in male impotence. Reason: Smoking leads to constriction of the blood vessels, which can in turn impede erections. In a recent study, 35% of men with proved impotence eliminated their problem simply by swearing off cigarettes for six weeks.

Source: *Sex Over 40*, Oak Hills Medical Building, Box 40428, San Antonio, TX 78229.

SEX AND ALCOHOL DON'T MIX

Excessive alcohol and sex don't mix for either gender. It's well known that an intoxicated man may have trouble attaining an erection. But recent clinical observation suggests that a woman often fails to lubricate after six or more drinks. And, although women may be more compliant when intoxicated, there's no evidence of increased sexual response or satisfaction.

RUNNING MAY BE BAD FOR YOUR SEXUAL DRIVE

Marathon men leave much of their passion on the road, according to a recent study. Men who run 40 or more miles per week were found to have 30% less testosterone and prolactin—the hormones required for male sexual drive. Theory: The lower hormone levels may explain why some runners have less sexual desire during intensive training.

HOW TO DEAL WITH INFERTILITY

• One of 10 American couples has failed to conceive after at least one year of marriage without contraception. Reasons: A rise in pelvic inflammatory disease (often caused by venereal diseases). Delay of child-bearing until the couple is older (and the woman is less fertile). Previous use of oral contraceptives (which delay pregnancies long after discontinued).

Source: *Journal of the American Medical Association*, 535 N. Dearborn St., Chicago 60610.

• Infertile women have long depended on unreliable blood tests to monitor ovulation. Better: Ultrasound—high-frequency sound waves that produce a TV picture. Using ultra-sound, doctors can determine the precise time to administer fertility drugs or artificial insemination. Results: In one study, five of 15 women with chronic infertility became pregnant.

Source: Study by University of Miami and Mount Sinai Medical Center, New York, reported in *USA Today*.

• Fertility problems (or outright sterility) affect 1.4 million American men. Recommended: Husbands should have a sperm count before their wives needlessly take birth control pills or have surgical sterilization.

Source: Dr. Cappy Rothman, a Los Angeles fertility expert, in *Nursing Life*.

• Male reproductive problems account for 40% of infertility. Basic problem: A 50% decline in the average American male's sperm count since the 1960's. Causes: Tobacco and marijuana smoking. . .X rays . . .zinc and vitamin C deficiencies. . .

exposure to toxic chemicals. . .stress.

Source: Dr. Sherman Silber, a fertility specialist at St. Luke's West Hospital, St. Louis, quoted in *Prevention*.

MALE FERTILITY AND VITAMIN C

Male fertility may be enhanced by a daily supplement of vitamin C. In a recent study, 35 men with fertility problems were found to have low levels of this vitamin. When 12 of them were given 500 mg daily supplements of vitamin C for 60 days, their wives all became pregnant. But of eight men given placebos and 15 untreated, none of the wives became pregnant. Theory: Vitamin C helps to normalize sperm movement.

Source: Study at the University of Texas Medical School, Galveston 77550.

INFERTILITY TREATMENTS MAY BE OVERRATED

• This was the conclusion of a study at a clinic in Halifax, Nova Scotia. Of the couples treated, 41% conceived within a year—but so did 35% who were diagnosed as infertile but decided *against* treatment. Bottom line: Before undergoing extreme treatments such as hormones or surgery, a couple should consider letting nature take its course.

Source: *New England Journal of Medicine*, 10 Shattuck St., Boston 02115.

Medical Problems

PROTECT YOURSELF AGAINST HOSPITAL BILLING ERRORS

When the mechanic hands you a bill for $500, it's unlikely that you'd pay it without a glance at the charges, but when given a hospital bill for $5,000, most people tend to do just that.

As it turns out, hospitals and doctors are far from infallible when it comes to billing. According to the New York Life Insurance Company, which has been auditing hospital bills for the past three years, the average hospital bill contains $600 worth of erroneous charges. This money comes not only out of the insurance company's pocket, but also out of yours. You can save money by knowing how the system works and how to spot billing errors.

There are many billing errors for the simple reason that many hospitals have inefficient billing systems. Major problem: Hospitals are geared to making sure that patients are billed for services provided, not toward verifying charges.

Typical mistake: Because of a clerical error, a $50 electrocardiogram is entered onto your bill at a $500 charge. Since you may not know the typical cost of an EKG, the error goes undetected.

Another example: A lab technician comes in to draw blood and finds that the patient is no longer there. However, he's still charged. Reason: Billing starts from the day the charges are entered in the book, and his charges are never cancelled.

Similar mistakes occur with drug prescriptions. Example: The doctor might order 10 days of penicillin and then switch to tetracycline after seven days. If the unused three days worth of penicillin is not returned, the patient is billed for it.

The four major mistake areas are:

1. *Respiratory therapy.* Equipment, such as oxygen tanks and breathing masks isn't credited when it's discontinued. Sometimes it's not even removed promptly from the room.

2. *Pharmacy charges.* Credit isn't given for drugs that were returned, or unused drugs that are not returned.

3. *Lab tests:* Cancellations of tests aren't noted.

4. *Central supply items.* Hospital staff or nurses may run out of something and borrow it from another patient. They intend to give credit or return the item, but often they don't get around to it.

What you can do:

• *Keep track of the most basic things,* such as how many times your blood was drawn. Suggestions: If you're able, jot down what happens daily. Note: If the patient is too sick to keep track of services rendered, a family member should try to keep track of the charges. Although it may be difficult to know how any routine things such as blood counts or X rays were done, someone who visits regularly is likely to know about non-routine services, such as barium enemas or cardiac catheterizations.

• *Ask questions.* Ask the doctor to be specific about tests. If he orders X rays, ask him what type of X rays. If he doesn't answer the question to your satisfaction, ask the nurse. Always ask. It's the most important thing a health-care consumer can do. Reassuring change: The newer generation of doctors is more willing to involve the patient in his own care.

• *Insist on an itemized bill,* not just a summary of charges.

• *Check room and board charges.* Count the days you were in the hospital and in what kind of room. Are you being charged for a private room, even though you were in a semi-private? Some hospitals have different semi-private rates for two-bed and four-bed rooms. Check your rate.

• Review the charges for TV rental and phone.

• Be equally careful with doctor bills. Often these bills are made out by the doctor's assistant, who may not be sure of what was done. Most common errors: Charges for services in the doctor's office, such as chest X ray or an injection, that weren't actually performed. Charge for routine hospital physician visits on days that the doctor was not in attendance.

Source: Janice Spillane, manager of cost containment in the group insurance department of New York Life Insurance Co., 51 Madison Ave., New York 10010.

MEDICAL INFORMATION UP-DATE

• Wallet-sized card records all your vital medical information on a microfilm strip. On an opposite corner there's a tiny magnifying glass. In an emergency, a doctor can bend the card until the lens is over the microfilm. Details covered: Major ailments, allergies, blood type, names of physician and others to contact, insurance numbers, baseline electrocardiogram reading.

For an application: Send a self-addressed, stamped envelope to National Health and Safety Awareness Center, 333 N. Michigan Ave., Chicago 60601.

THE SAFEST TRANSFUSIONS

• Private blood bank. Surgery patients at some hospitals can now store their own blood before the operation to ensure safer transfusions. Eligibility: Anyone who is free of anemia or blood impurities. The patient donates a pint a week to a blood bank, which freezes it until needed.

ASPIRIN: FACTS YOU SHOULD KNOW

• Aspirin overuse can lead to kidney damage, a recent study found. About 20% of patients on kidney dialysis may be there because of too much aspirin or some other analgesic. How much is too much? Two kilograms in six years—just three regular tablets a day—can seriously impair the kidney's cleansing function.

Source: Dr. William Bennett, Oregon Health Science University, Portland.

• Caffeine enhances the effectiveness of aspirin if you use enough of it. Earlier studies had concluded that caffeine does not boost the pain-killing properties of aspirin. Recent tests used 65 mg. of caffeine per standard tablet (double the amount of previous studies), which was found to increase pain relief by 40%.

Source: Study by the Rockland Research Institute, Orangeburg, NY 10962.

• Aspirin temporarily dulls the central nervous system, even when taken in small doses. Take this into account when engaged in an activity that demands vigilance.

Source: Study at Stony Brook School of Medicine, Stony Brook, NY, reported in *Prevention.*

SYMPTOMS OF TESTICULAR CANCER

Without prompt treatment, 29% of men who have testicular cancer will die from it. But virtually all could be cured if treated within a month of the onset of symptoms.

Recommended: Give yourself a testicular self-exam once a month. The exam takes only three minutes. It is best administered after a warm bath or shower, when the scrotum is most relaxed.

Technique: Examine the testicles separately, using fingers of both hands. Put your thumb on top of the testicle and your index and middle fingers underneath. Roll the testicle gently. (If it hurts, you're applying too much pressure.)

A normal testicle is firm, oval and free of lumps. Behind it you'll feel the epididymus (sperm storage duct), which is spongier.

Danger sign: A small, hard, usually painless lump or swelling on the front or side of the testicle. When in the slightest doubt, see a doctor.

Source: Dr. George Prout, chief of urology, Massachusettes General Hospital, in *Prevention.*

SUNGLASSES DON'T ALWAYS DO THE JOB

Ordinary sunglasses may fail to protect your eyes even if they feel comfortable and reduce glare. Reason: They don't screen out ultraviolet light, which has been linked with cataract formation. Most at risk: People with light-colored eyes, contact lens wearers and recent eye-surgery patients. For these groups, sunglasses with ultraviolet-ray filters are best.

Source: Dr. Richard Gibralter, ophthalmologist, Manhattan Eye, Ear and Throat Hospital, quoted in *Ladies' Home Journal.*

CHILDREN AND TOOTH DECAY

• Dentists are right—sugar is indeed a prime source of cavities in children. Researchers replaced sugar with natural fruit purees and sugar substitutes in the diets of 73 institutionalized children ages 5–17 for five years. Result: 53% of the children had no cavities. None were missing any permanent teeth.

Source: *American Journal of Public Health,* 1015 15 St. NW, Washington, DC 20005.

• Sealing children's teeth with a coat of plastic resin can reduce cavities by at least 50%. The plastic is applied to the molars, the most likely starting points for decay. It dries into a hard shield against plaque or food particles and lasts up to seven years.

Source: Studies by the National Institute of Dental Research, reported in *McCalls.*

• Tooth decay will be virtually non-existent among children and young adults by the end of the century. Coming soon: Cloning of the gene that produces tooth enamel. Lazer recrystallization of the mineral structure of decaying teeth.

Source: Dr. Harold Lee, director of the National Institute of Dental Research, Bethesda, MD.

DENTURE ADHESIVES MAY BE HARMFUL TO YOUR HEALTH

Denture adhesives can actually be more harmfull than helpful to users. Karaya gum, a common ingredient, is highly acidic and eats away the enamel of natural teeth. Constant use may dissolve bone tissue and promote fungus infections in the mouth. The good news: Properly fitting dentures don't require adhesives in the first place.

Source: Dr. George Murrell, University of Southern California, Los Angeles 90007.

YOUR ACHING FEET

• Foot supports are an answer to the ills of civilization, at least where aching arches are concerned. Our feet were designed to walk across the yielding surface of fields—without shoes. Instead, we walk on hard pavement, often in stylish footwear that doesn't fit correctly. With age, we lose muscle tone, and the problem becomes worse.

In time, the foot's ligaments and 26 bones go out of alignment. Nerves are pinched. Blood vessels are squeezed. Legs, pelvis and spine are thrown out of whack. It's an insidious process. Our body adjusts, and we don't notice the problem until our forties or fifties. Then we're distressed to find that we can barely walk without pain.

This is where custom-formed flexible foot supports come in. They return the foot to its natural position and function, or at least close to it. Slipped into any ordinary shoes, supports ease the shock of each step while at the same time maintaining the foot's normal flexing action. By easing unnatural friction, these devices can eliminate corns, bunions, callouses and hammertoes. In some cases, they even improve posture and balance.

Source: Harvey Rothschild, president of Featherspring International Corp., 712 N. 34 St., Seattle, WA 08103.

• Aching feet plague almost 75% of Americans over 18 years old—and 62% think it's normal for feet to hurt. Most commom problem: Blisters, calluses and corns. Women reported more pain than men, and 45% of the women said they wore uncomfortable shoes because they look good. But when asked if they'd give up style for comfort, 22% of the women said no.

Source: Gallup Poll.

• Shoe inserts help absorb the shock of your weight as it hits hard pavement. Only about one-eighth of an inch thick, the flexible polyurethane type can be cut to fit any shoe. Who needs inserts most: Women who wear business shoes with thin leather soles or heels higher than one and one-half inches.

Source: Dr. Charles Gudas, chief of foot surgery, University of Chicago Hospital, 950 E. 59 St., Chicago 60637.

PROTECTION FROM SOCIAL DISEASES

• Restroom reassurance. Although the risk cannot be entirely ruled out, researchers say there is no evidence that diseases such as herpes, hepatitis and gonorrhea can be contracted from public toilet seats or faucets. For extra security: Don't touch the toilet seat (use a seat cover or make your own from toilet paper). Avoid using the first few sheets of toilet paper. Flush with your foot. Most important: Wash your hands.

Source: Self, 350 Madison Ave., New York 10017.

• Though herpes dating services may help ease rejection and loneliness, they can also make participants sicker. Reason: There are several different strains of herpes. A person who has one variety can still be infected with another.

Source: Benjamin Raab, University of Chicago School of Medicine, Chicago 60637.

• Penicillin-resistant gonorrhea may soon be treated with a new drug called norfloxacin. This promising drug, which is still in the testing stage, has so far been 100% effective in curing gonorrhea in cases where penicillin therapy had not worked.

Source: Dr. Steven Crider, Naval Hospital, San Diego, CA, in New England Journal of Medicine.

• Urination within a few minutes after sex significantly reduces the chance of contracting venereal disease. Also good: Washing with soap and water. Dubious: Douching for women. It may force organisms into the cervix or mask disease symptoms.

Source: American Health, 80 Fifth Ave., New York 10011.

WHAT DOCTORS MAY NOT TELL YOU

Gallstone attacks occur randomly and cannot be prevented with a low-fat diet, new evidence indicates. Yet many physicians continue to prescribe such diets despite the futility of following them.

Source: Study by Dr. Michael Mogadam, Georgetown University, reported in Medical World News.

• Kidney stones may no longer require major surgery. With a new procedure called Percutaneous ultrasonic lithotripsy (PUL), a doctor makes a small puncture over the kidney and inserts a tube. Instruments are inserted through the tube to break up and remove the stones. Advantages: Less pain, a briefer convalescence and a 97% success rate. In the works: A technique using shock waves (transmitted through water) to break the stones into sand-fine fragments. The particles would then pass out of the body on their own.

Source: Dr. Joseph Segura, a urologist at the Mayo Clinic, Rochester, MN 55905.

• Ulcer relapses are less likely in patients who eat a bland, high-fiber diet. Bonus: Constipation, a problem in many ulcer patients, is prevented by the same high-fiber intake.

Source: The Lancet, 34 Beacon St., Boston 02106.

FACTS YOU SHOULD KNOW

• Huntington's chorea now can be detected even before its symptoms (nervousness and memory loss) appear. Result: Adult offspring of Huntington's parents can screen themselves to determine whether they're likely to pass the disease on to their offspring.

Source: New Scientist, King's Reach Tower, Stamford. St., London SE1 9LS.

• Curvature of the spine (scoliosis) now can be treated without surgery or bulky braces. ScoliTron, a device approved by the FDA, uses electricity to straighten the back. It sends short, painless impulses through the back muscles, causing them to contract, while the patient is sleeping. Note: Scoliosis afflicts one out of 10 children in this country.

Source: Intermedics, Inc., 240 Tarpon Inn Village, Freeport TX 77541.

• Brain damage can occur even without a direct blow to the head. Signs of trouble: Problems with memory and concentration. Or the victim becomes unstable, lethargic or easily fatigued without knowing why.

More information: National Head Injury Foundation, 18A Vernon St., Framingham, MA 01701.

• Blondes are seven times more likely to suffer malignant melanoma (a severe skin cancer) than people with black hair, a British study showed. Other melanoma links: Fair skin, heavy freckling, atypical skin moles, exposure to sunlight.

Source: *The Lancet*, 34 Beacon St., Boston 02106.

• New lice treatments: RID (by Pfizer) and A-200 Pyrinate (by Norcliff Thayer). Both are considered safer than those with even tiny amounts of DDT. Drawback: Because the new drugs are made with a natural insecticide from chrysanthemums, people with ragweed sensitivity could suffer an allergic reaction.

Source: *American Health.*

NEW FAT-REMOVAL TECHNIQUE

Suction lipectomy, in which fat deposits are vacuumed away, can reshape a body without scarring. Popular in France, the procedure was recently endorsed by the American Society of Plastic and Reconstructive Surgeons. Who can benefit: This is not for the obese. The ideal patient is generally trim except for localized bulges in thighs, buttocks or abdomen. Best candidates are under 40, when skin retains elasticity. Potential danger: Shock from fluid loss if too much fat is removed; loss of skin tissue; complications from poor postoperative care. The procedure calls for general anesthesia and often a brief hospital stay. Full recovery takes two months.

GOOD AND BAD NEWS ABOUT DRINKING

• Moderate drinking apparently does more than soothe jittery nerves. According to recent research, it also lowers chances of developing cardiovascular disease and gallstones.

Source: Study at the University Department of Medicine, Bristol Royal Infirmary, Bristol, England, reported in *The Lancet.*

• A single drink of hard liquor can lead to cardiac rhythm disturbances in chronic drinkers with a history of heart disease. Even healthy hearts can fall prey to "holiday heart syndrome"—arrhythmias that commmonly results from weekend imbibing. Bottom line: modest "social" drinking may not be as universally harmless as once thought.

Source: *RN*, 680 Kinderkamack Rd., Oradell, NJ 07649.

• Alcohol contributes to high blood pressure in hypertensive men. Those who regularly drink as much as 2.8 ounces of alcohol a day (about three drinks) can significantly lower their blood pressure by going on the wagon. And, according to research, a return to drink will bring levels back up again.

Source: Study at Dudley Road Hospital, Birmingham, England, reported in *Lancet.*

• Heavy drinkers tend to lose their ability for high-level abstract thinking—even when sober. Slightly tipsy (one drink beyond the usual daily quota) imbibers' thinking scores dropped dramatically. Drinking may take a greater toll on the mind than aging does.

Source: Research psychologist Elizabeth S. Parker, quoted in *American Health.*

LATEST WEAPON AGAINST SMOKING

Nicotine chewing gum was recently approved by the Federal Drug Administration for prescription use only. Aim: To help smokers kick their habit without new problems in nicotine withdrawal. Withdrawing from the gum is then relatively easy. Early returns: An English study found that more than 45% of patients tested were helped to quit. Caution: The gum should not be used by pregnant women or patients with heart disease.

MORE BAD NEWS ABOUT SMOKING

• Filters on cigarettes reduce smoke particles by 20%–96%. But as the cigarette shortens, the particle count increases. If one closes off the ventilating holes on the side of the filters with one's fingers while inhaling, the filter becomes even less effective. For example, with the vent holes blocked *Barclay* exceed unfiltered *Marlboro* in the number of particles inhaled.

Source: *Archives of Environmental Health*, 4000 Albermarle St., NW, Washington, DC 20016.

• Nonsmokers married to smokers are 54% more likely to develop lung cancer than those whose spouses don't smoke.

Source: Study at the Department of Environmental and Preventive Medicine, St. Bartholomew's Hospital Medical College, London.

• It's now common knowledge that pregnant women should stop smoking for the sake of their babies. But a recent study suggests that expectant fathers should follow the same rule. When Dad continued to smoke, the newborns showed significantly higher levels of thiocyanate (a tobacco smoke by-product) in their blood.

Source: Study at Cleveland Metropolitan General Hospital/ Case Western Reserve University, reported in *Glamour.*

• Persistent middle ear effusions (fluid buildup in the middle ear) are more common in children who are exposed to cigarette smoke. Exposure to three cigarette packs' worth of smoke increase the chance of infection four times. Children who are also predisposed to allergies or nasal congestion are six times as likely to have this problem.

Source: *Journal of the American Medical Association*, 535 N. Dearborn St., Chicago 60610.

• Preteens who smoke marijuana are risking their health more than older cigarette smokers. Reason: Marijuana contains more of some carcinogenic substances than tobacco does, and young lungs are especially vulnerable to the damaging effects of the smoke.

Source: American Lung Association, 1740 Broadway, New York 10019.

HOW TO STOP SNORING

Put a brick or two under both of your bed's pillow-end legs. Elevating your head will keep the airway open. Counterproductive: Using extra pillows. They'll only kink the airway.
• Avoid all depressants a few hours before bed. Take no alcohol, tranquilizers, sleeping pills or antihistamines late in the day.
• Lose weight. Three of four snorers are at least 20% over their ideal weight.
• Wear a cervical collar. It keeps the chin up and the windpipe open.
• Wear a "snore ball." Cut a small, solid-rubber ball in half. Using two patches of Velcro, attach the flat side of the half-sphere to the back of your pajama top. If done right, it should keep you off your back— the position for virtually all snoring.

Source: *Prevention*, 33 E. Minor St., Emmaus, PA 18049.

Staying Healthy

FITNESS VS. HEALTH

Considering the promotion of exercise over the last decade as the panacea for practically everything from heart disease to depression, it boggles the mind to look at the actual medical facts. Almost everything you've heard about the benefits of exercise in terms of health is *untrue*. Exercise is not only *not good* for your health, but it can be positively dangerous and even *fatal*. The only thing exercise will do for you is make you physically fit—fitness being defined as the capacity to do physical activity comfortably. But, contrary to popular misconception, *fitness and health are two separate things*.

There are three main myths about exercise and coronary health:

• Myth: Exercise makes your heart healthier. Many people, including physicians, have mistaken mechanical efficiency of the heart for health of the heart. Exercise *does* make your heart mechanically more efficient— it makes it possible to do more physical activity more comfortably. But your heart isn't healthier just because it's beating more slowly. This would be true only if each of us were allotted a certain number of heartbeats per lifetime. There is no such alotment. Some people in their nineties have had fast heartbeats all their lives.

• Myth: Exercise improves our coronary circulation. Everyone now agrees that this is untrue, even avid exercisers. Jim Fixx was the most dramatic example. His coronary arteries were badly clogged. The original idea that exercise improved coronary circulation was based on an early-1950's study done with dogs under highly artificial conditions. The tests had nothing to do with anything resembling human life. Also: Exercise does not stimulate your body to grow collateral blood vessels around the heart.

The only thing that does this is the clogging of your original arteries.

• Myth: Exercise reduces your coronary-risk factors. High blood pressure and cholesterol are the risk factors exercise is supposed to reduce. But. . most hypertension specialists would agree that the likelihood of reducing blood pressure to a significant degree via an exercise program is very small. A California study of trained distance runners found that they had the same range of blood pressure as nonrunners. Common misconception: That lower heart rate means lower blood pressure. One has nothing to with the other. It's been claimed that there are several types of cholesterol: HDL (high density lipoprotein), the "good" cholesterol. . .and the "bad" ones, LDL (low density lipoprotein) and triglycerides. Exercise supposedly raises the level of the good ones and lowers the bad. Problem: There's no proof that the "good" kind is really so good. The latest evidence suggests that even when your HDL goes up after exercise, it may be the wrong kind of HDL. Some studies show that HDL doesn't go up with exercise and that triglycerides and LDL don't go down. There's even an important study that shows the opposite actually occurs. So far, a low-fat, low-cholesterol diet is the only reliable way to lower cholesterol levels.

Other health myths:

• Myth: Exercise makes you live longer. No one really knows why some people live longer than others. Innumerable factors contribute to it, including genes, marital status, number of social contacts, resistance to stress and educational level. There's never been an unflawed study showing that exercise prolongs life. Just as many studies "prove" it as "disprove" it. The ones that make extravagant claims for exercise have gotten all the publicity. An interesting book called *Living to Be 100* analyzed 1,200 centegenarians. *Avoidance of stress* was a common denominator.

• Myth: Exercise makes you feel better. A lot of people do feel better when they exercise. But many other people would feel much better curling up with a good book. Although many claims have been made that exercise alleviates depression and anxiety, the data are contradictory. Some studies claim benefits, others don't. Some studies comparing the benefits of exercise with those of meditation and relaxation have found no difference.

The dangers of exercise: There is extreme danger to the heart during exercise. Eighty percent of sudden cardiac deaths occur during moderate or vigorous exercise. The sudden-death rate during running and among runners is seven to nine times greater than among sedentary people.

The most common danger of certain types of exercise, especially running, is orthopedic injuries. Podiatrists and orthopedists are doing a brisk business Every year two-thirds of all runners injure themselves sufficiently to have to give up running for a while. Worse: Today's runners may be tomorrow's arthritics.

There are other medical dangers to exercise. Intestinal bleeding is a common phenomenon among runners even after only a few miles. No one knows what causes this, but it's suspected to be something like gangrene—insufficient blood flow caused by diverting blood from the stomach to the muscles. You can bleed from the kidneys while running. Some runners develop asthma or other allergies, even if they've never had allergies before, and others develop intense constriction of the bronchial tubes. Young women are vulnerable to osteoporosis (brittle bones)—which usually affects only postmenopausal women. The loss of body fat is sufficient to alter their hormone systems.

What should you do? Don't engage in strenuous exercise. Among the risk factors for coronary disease, physical inactivity ranks near the bottom. You can counter this risk by getting a *little* exercise. Walking is the safest, easiest, least expensive exercise going. If you walk a mile twice a day at a pace of 20 minutes or less per mile, you'll surely get enough exercise to undo the risks of inactivity. Even a mile *once* a day is probably enough. That's all it takes to get the health benefits of exercise.

Source: Henry A. Solomon, MD, a cardiologist who practices in New York City, where he is on the faculty of Cornell University Medical College. Dr. Solomon is the author of *The Exercise Myth*, Harcourt Brace Jovanovich, 1250 Sixth Ave., San Diego, CA 92101.

THE BEST TIME OF DAY TO EAT

Diets work better when you eat more of your food early in the day. When six people consumed food worth 2,000 calories for breakfast and none for the rest of the day, they lost an average of 2.2 pounds in one week. But when they ate the same amount of food exclusively at dinnertime, four gained weight after a week and two lost relatively little. Theory: Calories consumed early in the day are more likely to be converted to energy than stored as fat.

Source: Study by Dr. Frank Halberg, University of Minnesota, cited in *The Health Letter*, Box 326, San Antonio, TX 78292.

STRESS ENDANGERS YOUR IMMUNE SYSTEM

Stress depletes your immune system. The extent depends on your individual personality. The production of *immunoglobulin A* (a virus fighter found in the saliva) was monitored by researchers at Harvard. They checked students during the first year of an accelerated program. Students in the test were divided into two personality types: (1) Those motivated by a need to be best and (2) Those motivated by a desire for close personal relationships. Every student's level of immunoglobulin-A dropped during the year, reaching a low during a particularly difficult exam period. The students driven to succeed had consistently lower levels of immunoglobulin-A throughout the study. Their opposites, who seemed to be more relaxed about the demands of the program, maintained higher levels.

Conclusion: The key to raising your immunity to disease may be learning to relax under pressure.

Source: *Science 84*, 1515 Massachusetts Ave., Washington, DC 20005.

HOW TO SIT CORRECTLY

Even if you have the perfect office chair, you can develop physical problems from prolonged sitting unless you align your body properly. Suggestions:
• Keep your neck and back in a straight line with your spine. Bend forward from the hips. Do not arch your lower back.
• Use a footrest to relieve swayback. Your knees should be higher than your hips.
• Move your feet up and down freqently to ensure constant circulation.
• Move your neck and shrug your shoulders to relieve the tension that results from prolonged sitting.

Source: *Office Hazards: How Your Job Can Make You Sick* by Joel Makower, Tilden Press, 1737 DeSales St. NW, Washington, DC 20036.

HIGH INTENSITY VS. MODERATE EXERCISE

Regular, moderate exercise is more healthful than more intensive but sporadic workouts, a comprehensive analysis confirms. Data from 66 studies show that a person lowers "bad" cholesterol and raises "good" cholesterol in proportion to the time spent in physical activity. But high intensity of exercise, by itself, has no effect. Bottom line: A brisk walk or slow job for 30 minutes a day is better than a heavy weekend out.

Source: Research at the University of Colorado, cited in *The Harvard Medical School Health Letter.*

THE BEST EXERCISE OF ALL

Swimming helps the entire musculature of the body, particularly the upper torso. It tones muscles (but does not build them). Greatest benefit: to the cardiovascular system.

For weight loss: Running is better than swimming. Reason: In running, the heat generated is sweated away, burning off more calories. Water, however, cools the swimmer. The heat is dissipated into the water, and fewer calories are consumed.

Best strokes for a workout: Crawl, butterfly and back strokes. They are the most strenuous.

Less taxing: The side, breast and elementary breast strokes. These strokes are usually used for long distances or for remaining in the water for extended periods without tiring yourself.

Applications: The elementary back stroke is best for survival. The face is clear of the water for easy breathing, and the limited muscle use saves energy. The side stroke is traditional for lifesaving. It can be performed with one arm, which leaves the other free to tow someone. It is very relaxing—and effective.

In swimming, the legs do not receive as much exercise as the arms and shoulders. To build up the legs: Hold a kickboard while swimming. This forces propulsion by the legs alone. Or swim with the flippers favored by divers. Their surface increases the resistance to the water, making the legs work harder.

Source: James Steen, swimming coach at Kenyon College, Gambier, OH 43022.

CANCER-PREVENTION DIET

• Eating less fat and more fiber has been reconfirmed as the best dietary defense against cancer. The American Cancer Society now joins the National Cancer Institute and the National Academy of Sciences in similar recommendations.

Besides cutting down on all fats (animal fats in particular) and eating more whole-grain foods, fresh vegetables and fruits for fiber, the guidelines also suggest eating: Less salt-cured, smoked or charcoal-broiled meat. More fruits and green vegetables (rich in vitamin C). Plenty of foods with beta carotene (a kind of vitamin A) such as asparagus, cantaloupe, carrots, spinach and tomatoes. More vegetables in the cabbage family—broccoli, brussel sprouts, cauliflower, turnips, watercress—and, of course, cabbage. They contain chemicals that inhibit cancer.

Bottom line: Researchers suggest that 35% of new cancer cases in the US could be prevented by proper diet.

• "Seed foods" such as beans and rice may help sever the link between red-meat diets and cancer of the breast and colon. How they work: The seeds prevent the body's enzymes from digesting meat protein. Instead of being absorbed by the bloodstream (a cancer factor), the protein is excreted. Other anti-cancer foods: Corn, potatoes and other high-fiber whole-grain cereals.

SALT WATCH

You should consume no more than 1,100–3,300 milligrams of sodium per day. (One teaspoon of salt = 2,000 mg.) Here's how to calculate the amount of sodium per serving, based on food-labeling regulations (mandatory next year).

• Sodium free: 5 mg. sodium or less.
• Very low sodium: 35 mg. or less.
• Low sodium: 140 mg. or less
• Reduced sodium: Usual level reduced by 75%
• Unsalted: Processed without salt when salt is ordinarily used.

Source: The National Research Council, 2101 Constitution Ave. NW, Washington, DC 20418.

HELP FOR THE AGING BRAIN

• Egg-yolk extract may help people with mildly imparied memories, according to recent research. The substance (active ingredient: lecithin) apparently makes aging brain cell membranes more flexible by displacing choleserol deposits. Another use for the extract: Easing the withdrawal symptoms of alcoholics and drug addicts.

Source: Research by Dr. David Samuel, head of the Center for Neurosciences and Behaviorial Research, Weizmann Institute of Science, Rehovot, Israel, in *Medical World News.*

• Vitamin C may help slow the aging process, doctors now believe. Mechanism: Vitamin C seems to combat oxidation (considered by many the basis of aging) at the cellular level. Note: Vitamin E also retards aging, but, unlike Vitamin C, it can be harmful if taken in excess.

Source: *New Scientist,* King's Reach Tower, Stamford, St., London SE1 9LS.

IN PRAISE OF TEA

Tea mimics the anti-depressant drugs. Its caffeine helps the brain synthesize chemical stimulants. Then its polyphenols help to keep those chemicals around longer.

Unlike coffee, tea doesn't raise blood cholesterol levels. It actually strengthens blood vessel walls and may even cut cholesterol absorption.

Rich in flouride, tea inhibits growth of decay-causing bacteria in dental plaque.

It's a good source of zinc, manganese and potassium, and its tannins help preserve vitamin C in the body.

Hot tea fights colds by doubling mucus flow, which helps to wash out germs.

BAD NEWS ABOUT CAFFEINE

• Caffeine and nicotine can interfere with high-blood pressure medications. Drugs (such as Inderal) used to treat high blood pressure work by reducing the amount of adrenaline in the patient's system. Caffeine and nicotine stimulate the production of adrenaline. Solution: Avoid cigarettes and caffeine-laden products. . .or consult your doctor.

• Too much caffeine can cause a loss of calcium and magnesium from the body. This presents a particular threat to women—who need extra calcium to prevent osteoporosis (a thinning of the bones) in later life.

Source: *Nutrition Research,* Fairview Park, Elmsford, NY 10523.

Personal Improvement

ALL ABOUT HAPPINESS

Sometimes happiness seems like a terribly elusive goal. We tend to forget that it doesn't come as a result of getting something we don't have, but rather of recognizing and appreciating what we do have. Some steps on the pathway to happiness:

• When you think about time, keep to the present. Research suggests that thinking too much about events far in the future or in the distant past leads to unhappiness. Very often those who are future-oriented tend to score very high in despair, anxiety, helplessness and unhappiness.

• Don't dwell on past injustices. You'll be unpopular company. No one wants to hear about how you got a raw deal in your divorce or how your boss doesn't appreciate you.

• Check your goals. Many of us get so wrapped up in the means that we forget about the ends. Ask yourself from time to time: "Why am I doing this? Am I working hard because I love my work, or because I think money will buy happiness?" Maybe you'd really like peace of mind or recognition or job satisfaction. These can be more immediate, attainable goals. If you're working yourself to the bone because you think money will eventually buy contentment, maybe you can discover that you don't really need a million dollars.

• Drop your bucket where you are. Legend says that an explorer's sailing ship was becalmed in the mouth of the Amazon River. Thinking they were in the salty ocean, he and the crew were dying of thirst. Out of the sky a voice commanded, "Drop your bucket where you are." They did so, pulled up fresh water and were thus saved. Lesson: Take advantage of what you already have. There are interesting, stimulating adventures waiting in your own backyard. Get to know your own children, for example.

• Develop the habit of noticing things. An active mind is never bored. Make a resolution to notice new things each day—about nature, people, or anything else that interests you. Ask questions. Don't assume you know all the answers, or that showing curiosity will be considered prying. Most people love to talk about themselves or their interests.

• Make some time for yourself. Everyone needs at least 20 minutes a day for quiet reflection—just thinking time. If you think while walking or running, leave the radio home. Let your thoughts drift to who you are, how you feel, what you're doing, how your life is going.

• Exercise. It's good for the mind. That doesn't mean jogging 10 miles a day. But a brisk walk, maybe during your self-reflection time, will put you in a better frame of mind. And it's important to do it regularly, as part of your daily routine, just as you shower and eat at certain times.

• Establish a regimen for yourself. This will give you a feeling of control. If you can stop smoking, lose weight, exercise, stick to a schedule, etc., you'll gain a sense of mastery. Anything that proves you can affect your own life will give you a positive sense of self.

• Listen to the old saw about accepting what you cannot change. As we get older, we have to accept our limitations. At some point in life, we all must recognize that we'll never be president of General Motors, a Nobel Prize winner, a *Time* cover subject, a perfect "10," or whatever else we thought was crucial to happiness.

• Learn to like yourself. The best way to think positively about yourself is to think positively about others. They will then reflect back to you how wonderful you are, which will make it a lot easier. Our sense of self is a reflection of other people's responses to us. Exercise: Pay three *sincere* compliments a day to others. You'll soon see how much better this makes you feel about yourself.

• Don't wear too many hats. Focus on one thing at a time. Make policy decisions ahead of time about situations such as taking work home. Set time aside for your family, yourself, your golf game, etc.—for having fun. If you set your priorities in advance, you avoid the anxiety of making moment-to-moment decisions. These priorities don't have to be carved in stone, but they'll help you cope. Also: If you stick to your plans, you don't have to feel guilty because you're having fun and not working.

• Keep your sense of humor. A good laugh goes a long way to making almost any situation bearable. It also lightens the impact of life's inevitable tragedies.

Source: Dr. Fredrick Koenig, professor of social psychology, Tulane University, New Orleans, LA 70118.

TO STOP UNWANTED THOUGHTS

The average person has more than 200 negative thoughts a day—worries, jealousies, insecurities, cravings for forbidden things, etc. (Depressed people have as many as 600.) You can't eliminate all the troublesome things that go through your mind, but you can certainly reduce the number of negative thoughts. Here's how:

1. When a negative thought begins to surface in your mind, pause. Just stop what you are doing for a few seconds. Don't say anything—talk will reinforce the bad feeling.
2. Take five deep, slow breaths. By taking in more oxygen you flush out your system and lower your level of anxiety. If you do this correctly, you will approach a meditative state.
3. Concentrate on a pleasant, relaxing scene—a walk on a breezy beach, for example. Take two to three minutes for a minor trouble, up to 10 minutes for a serious upset.

Best: Use this technique continuously un-

til the upsetting thoughts begin to decrease. Then practice it intermittently.

Source: Elinor Kinarthy, Ph.D., professor of psychology, Rio Hondo College, Whittier, CA 90608.

YOUR BRAIN POWER

• The brain works best in a cool room (65° Fahrenheit). Also helpful: (1) Diffused light (either natural or artificial light reflected from the ceiling and walls). (2) Upright posture, with the back bent slighly forward.

Source: *The Brain Book* by Peter Russell, E.P. Dutton, Inc., 2 Park Ave., New York 10016.

• Intelligence is more than verbal and mathematical abilities, according to a new theory. Hypothesis: The brain has six intelligence domains—musical ability, spatial skills, bodily talents and personal abilities, as well as language and logical reasoning skills. These different domains can work separately or they can work together. Note: Different "intelligences" seem to wax and wane at different times during a person's life.

Source: *Frames of Mind: The Theory of Multiple Intelligences* by psychologist Howard Gardner, Harvard University, Basic Books, 10 E. 53 St., New York 10022.

THE ART OF LISTENING

To really listen, switch off any negative thoughts about the speaker. Don't think faster than the person is talking. Start listening with the first sentence and concentrate on every word. Don't react to emotional words until you have heard the speaker out. Use facial expressions and body language to express interest and comprehension. Avoid the temptation to interrupt. Good question when the speaker pauses: "Do I understand correctly that. . .?"

Source: Nido Qubein, president of Creative Services, Inc., a business consulting firm, Box 6008, High Point, NC 27262.

SHARPEN YOUR READING SKILLS

• Speed reading is not a miracle. It is a skill that takes commitment, concentration and practice. Nor is it appropriate for all kinds of reading. Poetry, for example, was never meant to be whizzed through.

Good speed-reading courses employ a variety of techniques designed to make your reading more efficient and effective. The more you train yourself to use these techniques, the faster—and more productive—your reading will become. The basics:

• Pace your reading to your goals. Skim material from which you want only the main ideas. Go more slowly when you need to take in all the details.

• Concentrate. Reading is a mental process. If you are distracted while reading, you will proceed slowly and not remember what you have read.

• Use typographical clues to get the general content. Headlines, boldfaced lead-ins, bullets, etc. guide you through the material, indicating what you can skip and what you need to concentrate on most.

Specific tricks for gaining speed:

• Practice increasing your perceptual span —the breadth of type you can take in at a single glance. Force yourself to see more than a few words at a glance. Practice adding words until you can take in a whole column of type at once.

• Learn to recognize groups of words. Meaning comes from orderly groupings of words in sentences, not from individual words. Practice instant recognition of phrases without breaking them down into separate words.

• Use a finger to pace yourself. Trace a path for your eyes by running a finger under each line of type as you read it. Push yourself to go faster and faster with your finger. Your eyes—and mind—will follow.

• Check yourself for bad habits. Some people, for example, let their eyes regress before moving on to the next line of type. This wastes time, and you should make a conscious effort to stop it. (Rereading something you didn't under the first time is different and acceptable.) Another bad habit is subvocalizing—pronouncing words to yourself as you go along. This limits your reading speed to talking speed, which is much too slow for speed reading. Sound-

ing out new words also wastes time. Usually you can grasp their meaning in the total context of the sentence. If not, look them up.

Source: Robert de Vight, adjunct associate professor of communications at New York University and reading skills coordinator at Hofstra College.

• Reading regimen. Tear out magazine articles you want to read and put them in a folder with the newest items on top. Take the file with you everywhere so you can read the top item when you get a few spare minutes. Then mark the article for filing, throw it away or save it for the bathroom reading list.

Source: Ronni Eisenberg & Associates, professional organizers, 41 Central Park West, New York 10023.

• Breaks in concentration help you remember more from your reading. Best: A five- or 10-minute rest (both mental and physical) every 45 minutes or so, depending on the difficulty of the material.

• Memory aids. Exaggerate the idea...the more bizarre, the better. When taking notes, use outlining, bold print and color. When reading, underline key points. Emphasize the uniqueness of an idea or object.

Source: *The Brain Book* by Peter Russell, E.P. Dutton, Inc., 2 Park Ave., New York 10016.

HOW TO WIN AN ARGUMENT

• Key negotiation phrases:

Please correct me if I'm wrong. (Shows you're open to persuasion by objective facts ...defuses confrontations.)

Could I ask you a few questions to see if my facts are right? (Questions are less threatening than statements.)

Let me see if I understand what you're saying. (Once a person feels understood, he or she can relax and discuss the problem constructively.)

One fair solution might be...(Keep it open-ended and worthy of joint consideration.)

Let me get back to you. (Resist psychological pressure to give in right away.)

Source: *Getting to Yes* by Roger Fisher, Houghton Mifflin, 2 Park St., Boston 02107.

• Silence can be your best weapon in an argument or negotiation. If the other side makes an unreasonable proposal or attacks you personally, sit quietly. And if they fail to answer your honest question, just wait. The implied stalemate will force the opposition to come up with a better answer or suggestion.

Source: *Getting to Yes* by Roger Fisher, Houghton Mifflin, 2 Park St., Boston 02107.

• When you fail to win someone over, focus on what you can change (your strategy, effort, timing), not on what you can't (your basic personality). By taking a self-critical but constructive approach, you'll boost your motivation and activity level—the main prerequisites for success.

Source: Craig Anderson, assistant professor of psychology, Rice University, in *Self*.

PERSONAL HYGIENE TIPS

• The right soap is the mildest one that leaves your skin feeling clean. Never use a deodorant bar on your face. It only dries and irritates that sensitive area.

Source: *Harper's Bazaar*.

• Foot odor is caused by perspiration and bacteria. Antidote: Keep your feet clean and dry. Use talcum powder or cornstarch between your toes, and wear cotton or wool socks. Wear shoes made of leather or another material that "breathes." Let shoes air out for at least 24 hours between wearings. For persistent or very strong odor, apply an underarm antiperspirant to your soles.

• For healthy fingernails. Clip nails when wet (dry nails are brittle). Use an emery board to smooth nail surfaces, especially near the edges. Replace old nail clippers as they get dull. Fix breaks and cracks with nail glue (cyanoacrylate.) Never open a bottle seal or pull out a staple with your nails.

Source: Dr. Howard Baden, dermatologist, Harvard University in *American Health*.

• Skin workout. Do your heavy exercise before you shave to save your skin (perspiration can irritate clean-shaven skin). Use moisturizers and colognes after exercise, but always on clean skin. Wait for a few minutes after showering to apply powder or a deodorant (so that your skin will have time to dry completely).

Retirement & Estate Planning

THE BEST SOURCE OF RETIREMENT DOLLARS

Social Security payments contribute, on average, only 22% of the total retirement income of Americans 65 years old or older. Private pension plans contribute another 13%. Another one-third of retirement income comes from current earnings (either part-time jobs or self-employment income). The remainder is from investments. On average, investment income actually means more to retirees than either Social Security or pension benefits.

Source: The Investment Company Institute, 1775 K St., NW, Washington, DC 20006.

KEEPING TABS ON THE SOCIAL SECURITY ADMINISTRATION

Social Security payments received monthly upon retirement depend on both the age at which a person retires and the dollar amount of earnings credited to his account by the Social Security Administration. Problem: The SSA's records are not perfect and may reflect less than your earnings. According to the SSA, about $75 billion in earnings have not been recorded because they cannot be traced to any account. Personal protection: Obtain a copy of your Social Security earnings every three years, and review it carefully. Compare the figures against old W-2 forms. Clarify exactly which earnings were subject to Social Security tax. Best: If the records do not agree with the SSA's statement of your earnings, get in touch with your local SSA office immediately.

Source: Deloitte Haskins & Sells' *Week in Review*, 1114 Ave. of the Americas, New York 10036.

GOLDEN OPPORTUNITY FOR YOUR GOLDEN YEARS

There is a once-in-a-lifetime tax-free sale of a residence for those 55 and over. This can be done under the following conditions:
1. The homeowner is at least 55. (If a couple owns the home, only one need be 55 or over.)
2. The gain does not exceed $125,000. (If the gain is larger, the first $125,000 is tax free and the rest is taxed.)
3. The home has been occupied as the owner's principal residence for at least three of the five years before the sale.
4. The provision can be used only once in a lifetime. If it is used on one sale that produced a $90,000 gain, it may not be used again for the remaining $35,000.
5. It may not be used by a married couple if it has ever been used by either spouse, either when single or in an earlier marriage.

Source: *Tax Loopholes*, by Edward Mendlowitz, Boardroom Books, Millburn, NJ 07041.

SELF-DIRECTED IRAs

Manage-it-yourself Individual Retirement Accounts (IRAs) are a growing phenomenon. Individuals are increasingly using brokerage houses for their IRAs so they can decide where they will invest their retirement funds—and when. Aim: Flexibility, so that profits can be taken and funds can be switched into a more appropriate vehicle.

Added encouragement: When IRAs were first permitted universally in 1981, many banks and S&Ls offered outlandish interest rates of 17%, 18% and even 20%—high even in that period of steep interest rates. But those rates were a come-on, lasting only six months or a year. Many IRA investors were shocked the following years as the yield dropped dramatically. When the bank rates are in single-digit territory, there is added incentive for investors to choose a brokerage house or mutual fund with vehicles that have higher yields or greater potential. For instance, brokers can now offer IRA accounts with 30-year zero coupon bonds that give a higher rate than bank certificates of deposit. They also enable investors to lock in higher yields without having to reinvest the interest each year.

Advest charges an annual $30 custodial fee (billed in May) for self-directed IRAs. Although the custodial fee is tax deductible, it is difficult for an investor with only a $2,000 account to justify it. It is easier to justify the custodial fee when there is $5,000 or more in an account. And when the account reaches a significant size, the investor can buy a greater number of instruments and increase diversification.

With a brokerage house account or a no-load family of mutual funds, the investor who changes his mind about a five-year certificate of deposit pays an early-withdrawal penalty. But the only penalty for changing an IRA investment at a brokerage house is commission.

The big mistake made in self-directed IRAs is overtrading. Some people think there is a magical way for them to double their money in a very short time, especially in an IRA, and they buy highly speculative securities. Theory: Since they are playing with only $2,000, why not go for broke. But in volatile, aggressive stocks, investors can lose money at least as easily as they can make it. And any dollar in an IRA is worth even more to the investor than a regular dollar, since the money it earns is tax free. The account can turn into a sizable amount without risk. If you lose money in an IRA account, you get no tax help from the government—it gives you no tax deduction for such a loss.

Bottom line: Investors should not take chances with their IRA money. They should buy high-yielding instruments or equities

with the ability to pay a dividend (whether they actually do or not) and the potential for high growth.

Perhaps 5%–7% of IRA investors are traders who buy and sell all the time on their IRA account. They feel they don't have to worry about the tax consequences of taking a small gain fairly frequently, and they like the fact that they don't have to file a statement (so even their accountant doesn't see their losses and gains). No one is keeping score. It may even be recreational to some degree.

Conceptual error: Some people think there is more value to equities on a short-term basis than there actually is. Equities are really for the long term.

Source: Robert L. Thomas, executive vice president, Advest, 6 Central Row, Hartford, CT 06103.

WHO SHOULD OWN YOUR OWN INSURANCE POLICY

If you own the policy yourself, or if you retain any ownership rights over the policy at your death, the proceeds will be included in your estate and may be subject to estate tax. If your spouse owns the policy and you die first, the proceeds become part of your spouse's estate, subject to estate tax when he or she dies.

Strategy: Set up a trust for your children and let the trust own the policy. Make annual gifts to the trust to pay the premiums. The trustee pays your surviving spouse the income for life, and the principal, on your spouse's death, goes to the children. The impact of this strategy is to keep the proceeds out of both your estate and your spouse's.

Source: *Tax Loopholes*, by Edward Mendlowitz, Boardroom Books, Millburn, NJ 07041.

WHAT THE IRS SAYS ABOUT DEFERRED COMPENSATION

If an executive dies before receiving deferred compensation, the value of any deferred amount to which his or her family or estate becomes entitled will be included in the gross estate. Payments will also be subject to income tax when received. No reduction in estate tax is allowed for income taxes that may be imposed on future payments. If estate tax is paid on these amounts, the beneficiaries may be entitled to the limited benefit of a deduction for the estate tax attributable to income in respect of a decedent.

Source: *Retirement Magic: Tax Traps and Opportunities* by Peter I. Elinsky, Boardroom Books, Millburn, NJ 07041.

PITFALLS OF AN ORAL WILL

If you are tempted to tape record or videotape your will, don't do it until you check your state law on the subject. Most states won't accept a recorded will as valid because it lacks the handwriting and signature requirements. Unfortunate consequence: Your estate will be distributed as though you had died without leaving a will.

Source: *Estate of Reed*, 672 P2d 829.

LANGUAGE TRAPS TO AVOID

Words used to describe property left by a will have developed specific meanings. Recent example: An individual gave his neighbors his house, garage and household furnishings. Court's decision: The term *household furnishings* did not include the car parked in the garage at the time of the decedent's death or the contents of a safe inside the house. To be clear: Make detailed bequests, especially where money is involved. Courts have held that a bequest of the contents of a house does not include money, stocks, mortgages and bankbooks.

Source: *Re Estate of Baker*, (PA) 434 A2d 1213.

RELATIVES MAY NOT MAKE THE BEST GUARDIANS

In naming a guardian to raise your children in case they are orphaned, think twice before choosing family members. Grandparents, no matter how affectionate, may be unwilling or unable to resume childrearing. The same goes for your married but childless siblings. Best bet: Friends with children of the same age. Important: Always check with the persons you select before naming them in your will.

DEFERRED ANNUITIES SMARTER THAN IRA

With tax reform now in the picture, the insurance industry's deferred annuities are quickly becoming one of the most attractive investment products around...

Deferred annuities will serve as an alternative for individuals whose incentive to continue to make IRA contributions is greatly weakened by tax reform. Although contributions to a deferred annuity are not tax deductible, earnings do accumulate tax deferred. Advantage over an IRA: There is no limit to the amount of money you can invest in an annuity.

The new variable annuity could serve as the ideal replacement for investments that used to receive the benefit of favorable long-term capital-gains treatment. Reason: Long-term gains from investments in stocks, which are now going to be taxed as ordinary income, can be sheltered in a variable annuity. That income is not taxed until you withdraw the money.

How the annuities work:

An individual buys an annuity from an insurance company, paying a lump sum or a series of payments over time. In return, the insurance company guarantees that the funds will grow at a certain tax-free rate. Then, beginning on a specified date, the individual receives regular income payments for the rest of his life.

Payments depend on the amount of money contributed to the account, the length of time the funds are left in it, and the rate of return earned on the funds. Also a factor in determining the size of the payments is whether you include your spouse and other heirs as beneficiaries. Different options enable you to have payments continue to your wife, or to your children, or for a minimum of, say 20 years, regardless of who is there to receive them after you die.

Deferred annuities therefore can be considered part insurance and part investment. If you are willing to part with at least $5,000 (the minimum amount can differ from company to company) for five years or longer, you can be guaranteed a competitive, tax-free return on your funds. Because the earned income is not taxed until you begin withdrawing the money (presumably at a much lower rate tax rate), your funds accumulate much faster than they would if they were taxed. The insurance component, of course, is guaranteed regular monthly income payments for the rest of your life—taking the worry and risk out of budgeting for your retirement income. Also, should you die before you begin receiving payments, your heirs are guaranteed to receive the full amount of your original principal.

Source: Alexandra Armstrong, Alexandra Armstrong Advisors, Inc. 1140 Connecticut Ave. NW. Washington, DC 20036.

Your Money's Worth

CHOOSING A LONG-DISTANCE TELEPHONE SERVICE

Under the "equal access" program that is being implemented by local Bell Operating Companies, customers will be asked to choose which long-distance telephone service (either AT&T or an alternative company such as MCI, SBS or Sprint) they wish to use for making their long-distance calls.

Guidelines to help make the decision easier:

• Choose a service that offers the cheapest rates for your calling pattern. (Analyze your last year's telephone bills to see where you called, when you called, and how long you talked to each location.) If you are a heavy long-distance phoner, a company's minimum monthly charge won't hurt you. If you make few long-distance calls, however, the minimum charge might be more than your average telephone bill.

• Some companies also have minimum monthly usage requirements and/or volume discounts. Again, choose according to your needs. If you make only a few short calls a month you'll be hard pressed to justify the minimum. If you have high long-distance bills, a volume discount may offer big savings.

• Consider whether a company charges by distance or according to its service abilities in the areas you call most frequently. If you tend to call distant or hard-to-reach places, a "cheap" service with fewer connections may end up costing you more.

• Rounding off the number of minutes per call can add as much as 10% to your phone bill, especially if you make a lot of shorter calls. Check to see if the company you are considering rounds to the minute or to the tenth of a minute.

• Test each long-distance carrier that you, consider for line clarity and ease of connection.

There is still a big difference among services.

Source: *The Complete Guide to Lower Phone Costs* by Robert Krughoff, Consumers' Checkbook, 806 15 St. NW, Suite 926, Washington, DC 20005.

HELP FOR THE CONSUMER

• Home appliance help. A new trouble-shooting organization can help you get satisfaction if your dealer doesn't solve problems with your dishwasher, range or refrigerator. The Major Appliance Consumer Action Panel (MACAP) is a group of independent experts. It will route your complaints to companies, review any action taken, and follow up for you.

More information: MACAP, 20 N. Wacker Dr., Chicago 60606.

• To check the safety record of a product, call the Consumer Produce Safety Commission at (800) 638-2772. It provides three services: (1) Safety information—it will give you a list of features to check for on a particular product. (2) Product-recall information—you can find out if your particular model should be returned or readjusted. (3) Complaint registration—you record your problems with products, and the commission will notify the manufacturer(s).

• Product complaints can be made toll-free to more than 2,000 companies with 800 numbers. A list of some of these companies and strategies for getting satisfaction from manufacturers are spelled out in *How to Talk to a Company and Get Action.*

To order: Consumer Information Center Drawer 1734, Atlanta, GA 30301.

• Free help is as close as your telephone. A government booklet lists 800 numbers you can call for advice, information, and problem solving.

Source: *Direct Contacts for Consumers,* Consumer Information Center, Pueblo, CO 81109.

BUYING MEN'S SHOES

• Comfortable men's shoes feel slightly roomy but not loose on the feet. Toe box: high and rounded at the base. The space between your longest toe and the shoe tip should be the width of your index finger. Heel: Snug but flexible at the back, three-quarters of an inch to one inch in height. Soles: Crepe or rubber (better shock absorbers than leather). Buy shoes late in the afternoon, since feet tend to swell during the course of the day.

Source: *Gentlemen's Quarterly*, 350 Madison Ave., New York, 10017.

HOW MUCH "GOLD" IN A PIECE OF "GOLD" JEWELRY

Solid gold means only that the piece isn't hollow, not that it's "pure" gold. Gold-filled jewelry (look for the initials GF) has a 10-, 14- or 18-karat gold bonded to a metal base. Gold-plated pieces have a thin layer of gold on the surface: Gold electroplate is a relatively heavy coating. . . gold flash and gold wash are thinner.

WAYS TO PRESERVE VIDEOTAPES

Do not rewind your videotapes after use. Wait until just before playing them the next time. This flexes the tape and sweeps away any lingering humidity. Other safeguards:
• Store tapes in their boxes to keep dust and dirt from reaching them.
• Never touch the tape itself. Oil and acid from the fingers do damage. Also, cigarette smoke blown on the tapes does them no good.
• Avoid abrupt changes in temperature. When bringing a tape into a heated room from the cold outside, allow half an hour for the tape to adjust to the change before playing it.
• Never keep a tape in pause or still frame for more than a minute. The video heads moving back and forth will wear down that section of tape.

CARE AND FEEDING OF FILM

• Store film in the refrigerator or freezer if you don't plan to use it for a while. Refrigerated film can last one year past the expiration date. Film stored in the freezer will last up to two years.
• Mailing film to a photo lab saves you money on prints, but you run the risk of losing a roll. Precautions: Save one frame on each roll to photograph a card bearing your name and address. (You can carry the card in your camera bag.) Stick an adhesive label with the same information on each film cassette. Keep a record of the date you mailed the film and its subject matter.

Source: *Travel & Leisure*, 1350 Ave. of the Americas, New York 10019.

• If your film gets stuck in the camera, don't extract it in daylight. Ask a processor to remove the film in a darkroom, or do it yourself in total darkness. Technique: Remove the film cartridge. Pull the film completely out (by its edges). Then roll it up and place it in its original plastic container.

BUYING A USED COMPUTER

• Used personal computers are widely available at discounts of about 60% and can be a smart purchase for a company's day-to-day chores such as payroll updates. Other advantages besides a bargain price: Service is typically very good, and the best-known machines have a wide base of software available. For more advanced uses, though, a new machine is better.

Source: *Machine Design*, 1111 Chester Ave., Cleveland 44114.

• Check the screws on the back of the central unit. (Signs of wear will indicate frequent forays inside.) Watch carefully as the computer is turned on. (Major glitches often show up here.) Listen for systems diskettes that load smoothly and quietly the first time. Test each button of the keyboard in both upper and lower case, and then type a page of copy to test the printer. Is the warranty still in effect? (It is probably transferable.)

ACCESSORIES THAT ARE WORTH THE PRICE

Keyboard overlays for computer terminals eliminate the need to memorize long lists of control codes and key sequences. How they work: The plastic overlays fit right on the keyboard, with commands that are organized alphabetically. They're available for most popular hardware and software.

More information: Creative Computer Products, Box 85152, San Diego, CA 92138.

• Antistatic desk mat protects computer equipment from the hazards of static electricity. Includes a ten-foot grounding cord. Measures 24 inches by 26 inches.

Source: Sorbus Supplies Corp., 50 E. Swedesford Rd., Frazer, PA 19355.

Best software for transferring information by modem from your IBM PC to another computer (rated on ease of installation, learning and use; error handling; performance and versatilty) *Crosstalk XVI; Transend PC COMplete; Relay; Pfs:Access; Smartcom II; Omniterm 2; Crosstalk* requires 96K of memory. *Transcend* needs 256K. The others require 128K.

Source: *Software Digest Ratings Newsletter,* 1 Wynnewood Rd., Wynnewood, PA 19096.

SMART THINKING ABOUT COMPUTER REPAIRS

Extended warranties on personal computers make sense only if they cover the printer, keyboard and disk drive. If the policy covers just the computer, it's probably not worth the investment. Reason: A computer's central processing unit has few moving parts. It's the other components that are more likely to break down.

Source: *The Personal Computer Buyer's Guide* by Murray Bowes, Clarkson N. Potter, Inc., 1 Park Ave., New York 10016.

• Home computer breakdowns can run into big, big repair bills. Particuarlly vulnerable to glitches: Printers. Options for protection: A service contract from the dealer, an extended warranty from the manufacturer or an outside insurance policy. Example: Up to $2,000 of coverage on hardware and software for a annual cost of only $35.

HOW NOT TO GET CHEATED IN THE ANTIQUES MARKET

• Inspect painted antiques in sunlight so you can see if the texture and color of the paint are uniform. If they're not, the piece was likely repaired or altered. Also: Examine for wear in the right areas. For example, if a chair is authentic, paint should look worn on the top of the chair rails and seat crest.

Source: *House Beautiful,* 717 Fifth Ave., New York 10022.

• Frayed upholstery has little impact on the value of an antique chair or sofa. What counts: The age and condition of the frame. To check for authenticity: Look at the number of tack holes on the bottom of the seat frame. Several rows of holes indicate multiple reupholsterings—a sign that the chair has outlasted its fabric several times.

Source: *House Beautiful,* 717 Fifth Ave., New York 10022.

• Up-end an antique table to check its authenticity. Bad signs: An underside that's too smooth (indicates post-1850 machine planing). Holes from old screws or plugs (the top may originally have had a different base). Sharp edges (the top may be newly cut, even if made from old wood).

Source: *House Beautiful,* 717 Fifth Ave., New York 10022.

HOT NEW COLLECTIBLES

• Pre-1940 board games. Despite their scarcity, most can be found for $5–$30 at antique and collectible shows. Especially valuable: Games made by the Bliss, Singer, Sowden and Crandall companies.

Source: *Pop Culture Mania* by Stephen Hughes, McGraw Hill, 1221, Ave. of the Americas, New York 10020.

• Scripophily, the collecting of rare old stocks and bonds, can offer hobbyists a glimpse of industrial history and some beautifully engraved documents. Caution: With millions of old certificates in existence and relatively few collectors (only 3,000 in the US), you shouldn't expect to turn a profit.

Source: *Friends of Financial History,* 24 Broadway, New York 10004.